The
Transcendent
Life

OTHER BOOKS BY JIM ROSEMERGY

The Watcher

•

Living The Mystical Life Today

•

A Daily Guide to Spiritual Living

•

Even Mystics Have Bills to Pay

•

The Sacred Human

•

A Closer Walk With God

The
Transcendent
Life

Understanding the Nature
of True Power

AWAKENING

ACROPOLIS BOOKS, PUBLISHER
Lakewood, Colorado • Austell, Georgia

JIM ROSEMERGY

The Transcendent Life:
Understanding the Nature of True Power
©1998 by Jim Rosemergy

Published by Acropolis Books, Inc.
Under the Awakening Imprint

Printed in the United States of America.

For information contact:

ACROPOLIS BOOKS, INC.
Lakewood, Colorado

http://www.acropolisbooks.com

Cover design by Troy Scott Parker, Cimarron Design
Interior design by Bob Schram, Bookends
Author photo by Ken Clark

Library of Congress Cataloging-in-Publication Data

Rosemergy, Jim.
    The transcendent life : understanding the nature of true power /
Jim Rosemergy.
        p.   cm.
    ISBN 1-889051-25-x (pbk.)
        1. Humility—Christianity. 2. Spiritual life—Unity School of
Christianity. 3. Unity School of Christianity—Doctrines.
I. Title.
BX9890.U505R655 1998
241'.4—dc21   98-20155
                                                                         CIP

This book is printed on acid free paper that meets standard
Z 39.48 of the American National Standards Institute

ACKNOWLEDGEMENTS

Special thanks to Michael Krupp, Constance Wilson, and Carol Core of Acropolis Books for their commitment to bring to the human family a remembrance of a life of oneness with God.

The Transcendent Life
is dedicated to
all who believe that
God's Presence and Power
are called forth
by a humble soul.

Table of Contents

Writing *The Transcendent Life* forced me to put into practice its principles. I found that writing a book on humility was humbling. This, of course, does not mean that I am now a humble man. It means I have been humbled, and in the humbling I discovered something I believe is worthy of our attention.

I had a two month deadline for writing this book. I had written about humility before, so there was a wealth of material that served as my foundation, but I also felt called to come up higher. The call was to rise to a height where I could see what I had not seen before, but I felt the weight of my conditioning and past experience. It's hard to be humble, you know.

The transcendent life, the humble life, is hard because we make it hard. We hold on when the way to a new life is letting go. The things, experiences, and life that are truly ours come because we let go. Loving relationships come when we forget ourselves. We are lifted up by making ourselves small. It is in this way that we come to understand the true nature of power.

These are a few of the things I learned and put to the test. Putting principles to the test is the key because what I really learned was that ideas are not real until they are lived. *The Transcendent Life* was written with this in mind. There are powerful ideas within its pages, but there is also a section of the book entitled A Forty Day Guide to the Transcendent Life. I suggest you read and put to the test the exercises of each day. The basic message of this concluding section of *The Transcendent Life* is that the humble life is not principles and ideas. It is life, a life you are destined to live.

I sense a way of life unknown to most of us. We yearn and search for it, but for the majority of the human family, it is undiscovered. It remains what could be, a potential that tugs at our hearts and calls to us.

Creativity, compassion, and productivity are the fruits of this life, and their constant companion is a perceived effortlessness. Something comes into being, and it is apparent that its origin is not of the earth. It has the look and the touch of the divine. It is birthed in an unseen place but comes to life as it flows easily from within us. We say, "Of course, this is the way it should be. This is natural. It came without effort."

On the other hand, some things come into being through momentous effort. We hold them in mind and dwell upon them. We work hard and accomplish much, but often there is also much tension and anxiety. After the task is complete, we feel ourselves less instead of more. We are glad the project is over. We hope to never see it again. This is the way that has worn many of us out. In the coming age, we will discover not a way that brings things into manifestation, but a way of life that reveals our true selves and accomplishes the extraordinary work of Spirit.

I believe there is an insatiable driving force within us. Many of us respond to it by trying to improve the quality of our lives, but our greater desire is to live lives that express our spiritual identity. Tension, anxiety, and fatigue are not natural to this way of living. Peace is natural. Fulfillment is natural. Day by day, project by project, we feel ourselves more rather than less because our true identity is now present in the world.

There is power in us; there is compassion and love resting in our hearts that is beyond words; there is wisdom and creativity that will shock and enliven us and transform the world. The question is how are the power, love, compassion, and wisdom unleashed?

We wonder about the accomplishments of world renowned people. How do composers like Mozart creatively combine eight musical notes into masterpieces that move people for endless generations? How do writers and orators master language to such a degree that individuals who read their works are enlivened a thousand years from the day the words were uttered or written? For instance, why does the portion of Paul's letter to the Corinthians on love (I Cor. 13:1-13) touch the people of our age the same way it did the people of his day?

The physical feats of athletes challenge every generation, but always there is someone who runs the gauntlet and pushes beyond the supposed limits of endurance and excellence. People are even able to forgive and express love to those who have harmed them or their loved ones. Without a doubt, there is a potential within each of us that is destined to be released. The question is how.

Do you ever sit quietly and watch as great birds of prey allow themselves to be lifted by currents of air ascending a cliff or winds rising up a mountain slope? These masters of flight do not entertain a belief in personal power. Their "work" is not to rise, but to stretch forth their wings and be lifted by an unseen presence we know to be the wind. The birds can sense the rising air. They know its promise when it first brushes against their wings. Can you feel an ascending power in you? It has called you higher from the day you were born.

This power will one day be expressed in and through and as each of us. It awaits a sacred moment when we either feel or acknowledge our powerlessness or come to know that we know so little. The power is present. Love, compassion, and wisdom are present, closer than hands and feet and breathing. Through the ages only a few have known that these are unleashed by humility.

This insight is not new. Spiritual leaders of the past have always spoken of humility. For them, it was the key that unlocked the power within them.

Humility is the master key that is given to the human family. However, the humble life remains one of the least understood ideals to which we can aspire. It seems to make little sense. The people we see that appear to be most successful are certainly not humble. In fact, many speak highly of themselves and their abilities. How can powerlessness lead to the expression of power? What a paradox it would be.

This book explores humility and the paradox it presents to humanity. Humility is worthy of our attention because the promise is that through humility we can live a creative and compassionate life that flows effortlessly from a divine center within us.

Successful lives can be lived without humility, but the most extraordinary lives that have ever been lived were lived by people who were humble. The individuals we respect the most have or had humility at the center of their lives. Mother Teresa of Calcutta allowed a power greater than herself to pour through her soul upon the parched lives of people in need. Humility has allowed God's work to be done and an extraordinary life to be lived. The highest and best one of us can express is not to be a rarity. It is evidence of the way life can be lived. What is achieved by one is the destiny of the many. When one person runs a four-minute mile, a threshold is crossed inviting all milers to perform at this level. When one of us experiences the effortlessness that is the natural result of humility, all of us are called to live an effortless, highly productive life.

However, effort is a prelude to the effortless life. For instance, before a pianist can experience the harmony and rhythm of Rachmaninoff's Piano Concerto No. 5, much practice is required. There are insights along the way that build upon one another until finally the music seems not to be played, but birthed within the musician. It is the same when an athlete enters the "zone" and breaks a scoring record, but has little recollection of his or her efforts. There was only the flow and rhythm of the game.

The point is few if any beginners enter the zone. Effort is our beginning, but through humility we transcend the need to make it happen. We enter a special state of mind and heart that has always been our destiny. From this consciousness comes extraordinary accomplishments that are obviously expressions of Spirit.

We were made for this: love, compassion, power, and wisdom flowing through us for the common good. It is vital that as this begins to happen we do not lay claim to it and call it our own. Humility opens the door to this way of life, and it sustains it. Through humility, we are so in awe of what comes into expression that we cannot call it our own. We know that it transcends us. Something mystical has come alive. We have felt the touch of the Divine, and now it reaches out to touch the world.

CHAPTER ONE

THE SECRET REVEALED

POWER RELEASED

As a youngster, I felt the power that is at the heart of the humble life. A good friend and I were playing in a housing project under construction in Gretna, Louisiana. Large, deep holes had been dug, and because of the level of the ground water, the holes had filled with water. My friend Stan slipped into one of the pits. At first, I laughed as he struggled to crawl out, but then I noticed the slippery black mud that formed the sides of the hole did not allow him to obtain a hand-hold. He panicked, and while clawing at the muddy bank, he rose and sank several times in the murky water. Stan was in danger of drowning.

Without thinking, and without regard for my own safety, I slid into the hole and perched uneasily at the water's edge. As Stan surfaced, I reached out and grabbed him under his arms and with a strength beyond a young boy's lifted him straight out of the water and pulled him over me to safety. I did not realize it at the time, but I had felt the touch of the Divine and tapped a wellspring of Its power.

I never forgot the incident, but I never spoke about it. It remained a special memory of an unexplained phenomenon. Now, nearly forty years later, I understand what took place that day. Unknowingly, I touched the humility principle and experienced the touch of the Divine.

Many people share a similar special memory, for such events are not uncommon. Nearly every year, someone experiences a power beyond himself as he tries to help someone in need.

I once read of such an occurrence. A young wife heard a loud noise in the garage where her husband was working on their automobile. She flung open the door and saw her husband pinned beneath the heavy weight of the car. The weak cries of her loved one and his wide-eyed look of terror called the one hundred pound woman to action. She forgot herself and her limitations, and without a thought lifted the automobile from her fallen husband. Each year an account similar to this one is reported somewhere in our country. It is a blatant reminder of an untapped resource that lies within us.

Emergencies may seem to be the prerequisite before a transcendent power is available to us, but this is not true. Divine power is available in times of crisis, but it can also be accessed at any time and by anyone. In fact, a way of life awaits us in which special memories are natural and a part of daily living.

This is true because there is a humility principle constantly at work in our lives. ". . . for every one who exalts himself will be humbled, but he who humbles himself will be exalted" (Luke 18:14). Principles are powerful allies because they are eternal, dependable, and impersonal. The humility principle is as available to one person as another. It does not respect one race over another. It is not influenced by social or economic status or education. Its sole measure is intent. Why do we do the things we do? Do we work and live to be exalted or do we live to assist others and the unfoldment of the divine plan?

THE PARADOX

Our Creator is wise, for It has devised the universe so we gain respect and honor when it is not important to us. This is a paradox and the reason why many people have not yet discovered the humility principle.

This explains why hard work often goes unrewarded. Our motivation is narrow and limited to us. We are supposed to forget ourselves, but we have forgotten the people who share the planet with us. Rather than think about other people, we think about ourselves. We may not think or use the word exaltation, but we work to benefit ourselves. The paradox is that with every step we take, we fall behind. Furiously we try to claw our way to the top, but like Stan, our frantic efforts fail to lift us above our difficulties.

FROM EFFORT TO EFFORTLESS

This is an old story that is repeated again and again. From the human viewpoint, great effort must be expended before great works are accomplished. "Work hard and you will get ahead" expresses the work ethic of the late twentieth century. The problem is that in our age, it is obvious that hard work does not always lead to success. In fact, individuals are realizing that hard work is often prelude to frustration and exhaustion. Part of the problem is that the work is for ourselves. There is no humility or thought of the whole. Our intent is shallow, therefore we falter.

Much energy can be expended, but no work done. For instance, we can push against the wall of a tall building for hours and not move it a single inch. We are exhausted and perhaps frustrated, but by definition, no work is done because nothing is accomplished. A farmer can plow, seed, and, fertilize his fields, but unless there are crops to harvest, nothing is actually produced.

And there is another dimension to consider. The Hebrews built many colossal temples and structures in Egypt, but there was no great sense of accomplishment. How could there be? They were slaves. In pursuit of success, we sometimes become slaves to what we do. In fact, hard work can lead to fatigue if it is not joined to a purpose that reaches beyond ourselves.

Whether we work hard and accomplish little or work hard and accomplish much but feel like a slave to our work, there is another way. Remember, the humble life is marked by a feeling of effortlessness. In fact, because of this feeling and the ease of accomplishment, we cannot call the achievement our own. Taking credit, exalting ourselves, is obviously an error. The effortlessness with which something unfolds and the extraordinary results tell us that a power greater than ourselves is at work.

David's Exaltation

Understanding the humility principle enables us to work in harmony with it. We can adopt it in a certain situation and eventually as a way of life. The Bible is filled with examples of this approach to living. Not only does scripture tell the tale of the power of humility, it also reveals how the humility principle is activated. The story of David and Goliath is a good place to start our study of the humble life. Let us return to the time David stood before Goliath and heard the giant's thundering voice shout to him of how the birds would soon eat his flesh. David replied, "You come to me with a sword and with a spear and with a javelin; but I come to you in the name of the Lord of hosts, the God of the armies of Israel, whom you have defied. This day the Lord will deliver you into my hand . . ." (I Samuel 17:45-46).

David's words were an indication of humility. As he stood before the Philistine champion, David did not rely upon his skill with the sling, although it was considerable, nor did he look back at his previous triumphs over the lion and the bear. David's confidence was not in himself. His confidence was in God, and because of this, an extraordinary event happened. The seemingly impossible came into being.

This confrontation is a perfect out-picturing of the humility principle: ". . . for everyone who exalts himself will be humbled, but he who humbles himself will be exalted." This was critical for David. If his confidence had been in himself, he would most likely have died a foolish boy facing a man of war.

Goliath activated the humility principle by exalting himself and caused the forces of the universe to bring him to his knees. In this instance, the force called upon was David, Israel's boy champion, who humbled himself by acknowledging the power and presence of God. He knew that by himself he could not defeat Goliath. David's humble spirit allowed a supreme power, wisdom, and calm to be expressed through him.

David's humility can be our teacher. He spoke the truth of God's power and so can we. There is, however, no power in the words themselves. The words spoken by David allow us to catch a glimpse of the consciousness of humility and learn more of its ways.

Several ideas are obvious in David and Goliath's story. When we face a challenge head-on, acknowledging Spirit's power and giving God the credit before we act, power is unleashed from within us. Our efforts are necessary, for God and we are at work together. Our actions are guided by infinite wisdom, and therefore not our own. In an effortless way, what is needed in that moment is available to us.

A secret is revealed: the humility principle. As we examine the life that naturally flows when we humble ourselves, we will see many examples of the touch of the Divine. Each touch is a gift. Sometimes we are given words to say. At other times, our efforts are guided, and we do the right thing. All of this and more occurs without us taking thought. Effortlessly, we face our challenges, live life, and learn beyond all doubt that we are not alone, that our God loves us and is in oneness with us always.

KEY IDEAS

1. There is a humility principle at work in my life. He who exalts himself will be humbled, and he who humbles himself will be exalted.
2. One sign of humility is effortlessness.
3. Forgetting myself and my limitations and serving the needs of another are forms of humility.
4. Acknowledging the presence and power of God is a form of humility.

AFFIRMATION

I acknowledge my powerlessness and the power God is.

SUMMARY

Humility invites the love, compassion, and power God is to come into expression.

CHAPTER TWO

FROM THE ORDINARY TO THE EXTRAORDINARY

HUMBLE BEGINNINGS

The secret is revealed, ". . . for everyone who exalts himself will be humbled, but he who humbles himself will be exalted (Luke 18:14). We have seen this principle at work. David knew his powerlessness and instead of choosing fear, he chose to acknowledge the power of God and to open himself to it. He knew that without the touch of the Divine, he could not conquer the Philistine. This is the essence of humility. We feel powerless, and rather than allow this feeling to conquer us, we humble ourselves and become avenues for spiritual forces. Oddly, it is our powerlessness that makes the power of God more real and us more receptive to it.

David trusted his life to the humility principle, and we, too, can place our lives in Humility's hands as we face the giant difficulties that threaten our well-being. David must have appeared weak to Goliath, just as humility appears docile to most of humanity, but it is a consciousness of quiet strength from which to calmly and triumphantly live life. When we are humble, we can face our Goliath, for humility allows us to become sensitive to the gathering of spiritual forces. They are always present, but when we know that we of ourselves can do nothing, we can first feel and then express the power that God is.

Forgetting ourselves and thinking of others is often enough to activate the mighty forces of Spirit. This was evident in the story of the woman who was able to lift an automobile off her husband. Self-forgetting is a form of humility; no longer are we the center of our world. Because of this, divine forces which have made a home in us can rise up to greet the challenge that is at hand.

HUMILITY INVITES TRANSFORMATION

We may let go of selfishness in a time of crisis, but in the course of an ordinary day, we have the opportunity to remember others and forget ourselves. We can praise and give thanks for the contribution that others make to our workplace, our personal lives, and our world. This may not be the fullness of humility, but it is a step in the right direction. Anything that gives positive attention to someone other than ourselves begins to build a consciousness of humility in our souls.

The humility principle can fortify us in times of crisis, but it is also a powerful ally during the course of an ordinary day. In fact, humility can transform the ordinary into the extraordinary.

In the story of the wedding at Cana (John 2:1-11), Jesus illustrates the transforming power of humility. As we join this episode in Jesus' life, it is the third day of a wedding feast. In biblical days, it was natural for a wedding celebration to continue for many days. As the revelry begins, the most honored guests are seated next to the groom. Those of lesser prestige are seated farther away. In addition, the best wine is served by the most celebrated guests on the first day of the festivities when everyone is sober, and the poorer quality wine is provided as the days go by.

It was the third day, and Jesus' time to supply the wine had not yet come. Obviously, he was not one of the honored guests. However, Jesus assumed a humble position at the wedding even though he had power and dominion over cosmic forces. As we shall see, it is this humble consciousness that releases a power that transforms the ordinary into the extraordinary.

When Jesus' time came to furnish the wine, he asked that six stone containers be filled with water and the contents served to the wedding party. Miraculously the water had been transformed into wine. ". . . the steward of the feast called the bridegroom and said to him, 'Every man serves the good wine first; and when men have drunk freely, then the poor wine; but you have kept the good wine until now'" (John 2:9-10). Humility served as a doorway, so the ordinary, the water, could be transformed into the extraordinary, the wine.

Imagine what would have happened if Jesus had exalted himself and taken the place of honor at the feast. The steward would have asked him to rise in front of all the guests and take a seat farther from the groom. Jesus would have been humiliated, but more importantly, he would not have been an avenue for God's transforming power. Instead, Jesus humbled himself, and once again the Presence had an avenue through which to do Its work.

Humility, A Choice

Humility begins as a choice. We have the same choice Jesus had at the wedding at Cana. We can seek the seat of honor or wait until our time comes. If we wait in humility and acknowledge the power God is, the ordinary can become the extraordinary. Life will taste different. Ordinary events will become sacred. Simple things will become precious. We will be less prone to consider some happenings grand and others mundane. Humility lifts the scales from our eyes, so we can see the world from the highest point of view.

Each day we have the opportunity to be humble, but more than this, we have the opportunity to live in humility. Because of some limitation, we may appear to be destined to live an ordinary life without the promise of success, but this is not true. For instance, I know a woman who has been blind most of her life, but she sees clearly. She has refused to be restrained. She is a musician who speaks eloquently to children and adults about how anyone can rise above a seeming handicap. In fact, her blindness has helped her discover inner qualities of persistence and determination that sighted people often fail to see in themselves.

Any handicap or limitation humbles us. Initially, we feel a certain sense of powerlessness. There are things we cannot do. The question is will we be bitter and resentful of others and their abilities or will we humble ourselves so Spirit can lead us to the discovery of our capabilities and inner strength? We may not be able to do all the things that others do, but we can allow the Presence to make something of our lives regardless of our supposed limitation.

Being humbled can make us blind to the joy of life, or it can help us see. We must choose how we experience our limitation or sense of powerlessness. We can become impotent, or we can come to know a power greater than ourselves that can pour through us into our world and the greater world in which we dwell.

Terry Fox chose to live in the greater world. Terry lost a leg to cancer. The loss humbled him; however it did not make him bitter; it made him better. He called upon a power greater than himself as he began a strenuous journey across Canada. Mr. Fox decided to walk from shore to shore collecting funds for cancer research. With every painful step he took, he walked in a larger world. He lost a leg, but that loss enabled him to find qualities within himself that he did not know existed. Spirit lifted him and held him high, so we could see how powerful a humble person can be.

Our experiences help us realize that there are many things we cannot do alone. A simple healing need can reveal the path to humility. The question is will we walk the path? All the medical technology and discoveries of a hundred years cannot help us when we are caught in the grip of the common cold. We are humbled, but will we humble ourselves? Will we acknowledge our powerlessness and a power greater than ourselves? If we are able to make ourselves small, the ordinary can become the extraordinary.

HUMILITY—TO MAKE SMALL

The subtlety of another event in Jesus' life demonstrates how humility can shield us from harm and provide us with what is needed to face a difficult situation. In the eighth chapter of John, there is an account of a woman caught in the act of adultery. Trembling with fear, she was brought to Jesus by the Scribes and Pharisees. They want to know what to do with her. Their question tests Jesus' respect for and adherence to Jewish law because the law demands that the woman be put to death. Jesus knew the law and that they were prepared to carry out the sentence.

Jesus made himself small by bending down and writing on the ground. The physical act of stooping denotes humbling oneself. This is needful because it would not be healthy to stand and argue with a group of men who intend to kill the woman. The humility principle was at work in Jesus and from his humble position he spoke, "Let him who is without sin among you be the first to throw a stone at her" (John 8:7).

Making oneself small and non-resistant is an act of humility. Whenever we choose to act this way, we invite the power of God to lift us up. The Presence and Power express Themselves in varied ways. In this instance, Jesus' wise words to the religious leaders saved the woman's life, and ultimately she was transformed. The words were evidence of the touch of the Divine.

I believe no thought was taken as to how to handle the crisis. There was no time for thinking. Instinctively, Jesus made himself small and his simple act resulted in divine wisdom flowing from his lips. They were the perfect words, perhaps the only words that could have caused the men to drop their stones, turn, and walk away.

A story such as this one stresses the need for humility and illustrates how quickly Spirit can act through someone who has made himself small. In an instant, we can be touched by the Divine. There is no other need than to be humble.

KEY IDEAS

1. Humility transforms the ordinary to the extraordinary.
2. The humble life begins as a choice.
3. Humility allows me to see the sacred in simple things.
4. Humility can shield me from harm.
5. Wisdom is one of the fruits of humility, evidence of the touch of the Divine.
6. Being humbled can make me blind, but it can also help me see.
7. Each day I have the opportunity to live in humility.

AFFIRMATION
I trust my life to the humility principle.

SUMMARY
This is the beginning of power: I of myself can do nothing.

CHAPTER THREE

THE MYTH OF PERSONAL POWER

HE WHO EXALTS HIMSELF . . .

He who humbles himself will be exalted. . . .We have seen a number of examples of this principle at work. Humility opens the gateway of our souls, so physical power can be expressed. It is also an avenue for divine wisdom. With humility, work can be performed effortlessly. In addition, creativity is a gift of humility. There are myriad ways in which we can be exalted through the humility principle. However, when we exalt ourselves we activate the humility principle, and we are humbled.

Saul, a member of the smallest tribe of Israel and its first king, began in humility. He was reluctant to assume the role of king, but the prophet Samuel anointed him, and his tragic reign began.

The life of Saul vividly illustrates that a sense of personal power and accomplishment are prelude to attempts to exalt ourselves. We may never say the words, but our inner thoughts are, "Look what I have done."

Saul was taller than the other men of Israel and was a fearless warrior. As his dominance of the Philistines became known, the people rallied around him. The victories pleased the people, but Saul's failure to follow God's guidance created a sense of separation from God.

When we are first estranged from the Presence, we are not aware of it. We are like the branch that has fallen from the tree. We are green, and the fruit may still cling to the branch, but our demise is imminent. The modern image of this human dilemma is a light running on a battery rather than being connected to the city's source of electrical energy. At first, the light burns brightly, but soon its brilliance fades. This is the way it was with Saul.

The fading of Saul's light began when he failed to follow the prophet Samuel's instructions. In I Samuel 10:8, the prophet says to Saul, "And you shall go down before me to Gilgal; and behold, I am coming to you to offer burnt offerings and to sacrifice peace offerings. Seven days you shall wait, until I come to you and show you what you shall do."

Saul waits in Gilgal the appointed seven days, and when Samuel does not come, the warrior king performs the religious rites. Just as he completes the offerings, Samuel arrives and asks Saul what he has done. The king, filled with excuses, replies, "When I saw that the people were scattering *from me*, and that you did not come within the days appointed, and that the Philistines had mustered at Mishmash, I said, 'Now the Philistine will come down *upon me* at Gilgal, and I have not entreated the favor of the Lord'; so I *forced* myself, and offered the burnt offering" (I Samuel 13:11-12).

NOT BY MIGHT, BUT BY SPIRIT

The truth is that Saul feared for his life because the people were leaving him, and the enemy was amassing for battle at Mishmash. He stated that his motivation was that he must entreat God's favor through offerings, but his faith was in numbers of warriors rather than God. He did not have the insight discovered by Zechariah. "Not by might, nor by power, but by my Spirit . . ." (Zechariah 4:6). When we believe in personal power, we experience fear. The reason is simple: We have placed our faith in ourselves rather than the transcendent power that God is.

This is the first example of Saul's sense of personal power and accomplishment. He made the mistake we all make when he assumed that there was something he could do that would gain favor with God. The truth is we have God's favor, and it is experienced not through human effort, but through grace, humility, and the realization that we of ourselves can do nothing. This episode in Saul's life is significant because it reminds us how we try to not only make things happen in our human lives, but, also, in our relationship with Spirit.

In a second illustration of disobedience and lack of spiritual understanding, Samuel tells Saul that he is to utterly destroy an enemy of Israel. "Now go and smite Amalek, and utterly destroy all that they have . . ." (I Samuel 15:3). This is classic Old Testament symbology. To the literalist, this verse indicates a vengeful God. To the individual who sees symbolism in Bible stories, there is another perspective. This seemingly harsh instruction from the prophet reveals an important insight into a process of spiritual growth. That which stands between us and the unification of the spiritual aspects of our being must be utterly destroyed or released from our consciousness. Literally, Saul's basic purpose was to unify the fiercely independent tribes of Israel, but symbolically his life's purpose mirrors our need to unify the spiritual dimensions of our being.

We experience our own battles just as the Hebrews fought hand to hand against their enemies, except our enemies are of our own household. For instance, our battle is against resentment and condemnation of others. Obviously, these unwholesome parts of our souls must be cleansed before God's love can unify us with our fellow human beings, the earth, and even the distant galaxies.

15

Saul failed to follow the instructions given to him. Instead, he retained the best of Amalek's sheep and oxen. When Samuel confronted him, Saul's excuse was that the animals were to be sacrificed to the Lord. Notice that this event is similar to the previous happening. Once again it is evident that Saul believes that he can gain God's favor through his personal actions. He remains unaware that he already has God's love. To the king's excuses Samuel answered, "Has the Lord as great delight in burnt offerings and sacrifices, as in obeying the voice of the Lord? Behold, to obey is better than sacrifice . . ." (I Samuel 15:22).

On the surface, Saul's transgressions seem slight, but they are symbolic of the actions of personal will and a sense of personal power. The king's behavior also indicates that he thought there were things that he could personally do that would deepen his relationship with God. How many human beings have believed this lie? Nothing we can do or will ever do changes Spirit's deep love for us. The Presence withholds nothing because the Presence does not withhold Itself from us. If we have been like Saul thinking that through doing we draw near to our Creator, it is time to cease our good deeds and become still enough for us to hear the voice still and small tell us of God's everlasting love.

Saul remains king of Israel, but his fortunes change drastically. The humility principle is at work in his life. David, the shepherd who defeated Goliath becomes a great warrior. The people shout, "Saul has slain his thousands, and David his ten thousands" (I Samuel 18:7). Saul's personal will and sense of personal power lead to feelings of jealousy and eventually rage toward the people's new hero. The king tries to kill David, but to no avail. Finally, Saul, defeated in battle, falls on his own sword and ends his tragic life.

His sense of personal power led him to a feeling of total powerlessness. This could have been a new beginning. The king was humbled, but he failed to humble himself. If he had done so, the story would have ended differently.

The assertion of personal will and power is a form of exaltation that activates the law: ". . . for every one who exalts himself will be humbled . . ." (Luke 18:14). The end result is the realization that the human will is weak, for it cannot accomplish what we would like it to achieve. We understand how powerless we are, for our dreams and goals go unrealized, and like Saul, there is nothing we can do to make them come true.

A MODERN EXAMPLE

Years ago, I attended a baseball game in Kansas City. A young, talented rookie pitcher entered the game. During the course of the few innings he pitched, I saw the power of humility at work as well as the folly of exaltation. The pitcher would strike out one batter and strut around the mound enjoying his accomplishment. The next batter would drill the ball off the outfield wall or at least hit safely, and the pitcher would be humbled. The next batter would be handled easily. The strutting would occur, and the following batter would hit safely. On and on the cycle went, an example of the humility principle at work.

FROM POWERLESSNESS TO ALL POWER

The evening at the stadium in Kansas City will not be remembered as a grand example of the humility principle, but there was a man of ancient times who began in self will and exaltation and grew in humility—Saul of Tarsus who became Paul the Apostle. Saul hated the followers of Jesus, and he obtained authorization allowing him to capture the early disciples. He was filled with hatred and a sense of personal power and will. He thought he knew what was right. On the road to Damascus, he was blinded and had to seek the help of Ananias, one of the followers he would have imprisoned or put to death.

Saul became so powerless that he was unable to accomplish the simplest thing for himself. This humbled him. For three days, he was without sight and did not eat or drink. In this humble state, the power of God transformed Saul, and he became Paul the Apostle, the great advocate of the Christ life.

The beginning was willfulness, for he was filled with zeal for his religion and for God. He was willing to do a great work, but it was his work, not God's. He failed to comprehend the inner meaning of Psalm 127:1, "Unless the Lord builds the house, those who build it labor in vain." On the road to Damascus, Saul began to see the folly of the pursuit of spirituality through one's will.

Jesus stressed this same idea when he said, ". . . the kingdom of heaven has suffered violence, and men of violence take it by force . . ." (Matthew 11:12). Literally, this verse refers to the fact that the zealots of Jesus' day wanted to overthrow Rome and establish the kingdom of God on earth. Obviously, a spiritual kingdom cannot come into being through physical force. Symbolically, this is an important message for those of us who attempt to succeed in spiritual matters by using the same methods we have used in business or in earthly endeavors. The will is strong, and we believe it is our ally in our spiritual quest. We are misguided and as yet do not understand that Spirit's plan unfolds through humility.

Paul grew to understand this ideal. To the Corinthians he wrote, "Let him who boasts, boast of the Lord" (II Corinthians 10:17). In Galatians 2:20, he reveals the heart of the humility principle and its ultimate conclusion, ". . . it is no longer I who live, but Christ who lives in me . . ." The one who had been willful states in the letter to the Philippians, ". . . for I have learned, in whatever state I am, to be content" (Philippians 4:11).

Humility leads to supreme contentment. The Spirit of God in us that rests in silent repose comes to life. We are a new creation, one willing to be of service to the One.

HUMILITY'S FOUNDATION

Humility is based on the truth that there is only one Presence and one Power—God. When we claim power as our own, we believe a lie, and when a lie is the premise upon which we live our lives, we are deceived. It is like a magician who holds a box for us to see and says, "See this empty container . . ." We nod our heads, and the trick is on. We have accepted the obvious, and it is a lie. The box is not empty.

In truth, there is no personal power. There is only one power—the power God is. The humble life is not one of using or wielding divine power, but allowing it to use us. Let us become servants of the power, rather than trying to master it or claim it as our own. Such an attempt ends in powerlessness; however the wonder of this condition is that it is a place from which God can lift us up.

It is as Jesus stated, "My teaching is not mine, but his who sent me; if any man's will is to do his will, he shall know whether the teaching is from God or whether I am speaking on my own authority. He who speaks on his own authority seeks his own glory; but he who seeks the glory of him who sent him is true, and in him there is no falsehood" (John 7:16-18).

It is best not to seek glory for ourselves because if we do, the law will bring us to a position where we have no sense of personal power. From this place of powerlessness, all the power that is God can be expressed in and through us. We have only to realize our helplessness, turn Godward, and allow ourselves to be lifted up. This is humility. We are like the bird flying near the cliff that is suddenly lifted by an unseen, rising current of air. The lifting is effortless, and from our new height we see what we have never seen before.

Can you see the cycle? We begin under the false assumption that we have power. Our life is based on this lie, and eventually we confront some difficulty that illustrates to us that we are powerless. In fact, this condition or situation may appear to have established itself as the power in our lives. From this powerless and sometimes helpless consciousness, we are candidates for a new way of living. If we humble ourselves and acknowledge our powerlessness, the power God is will begin to express Itself in and through and as us. This is a grand cycle, one that is often quite painful, but the good news is that true power is often discovered when we feel least powerful. It is as the scripture says, ". . . for my power is made perfect in weakness" (II Cor. 12:9).

KEY IDEAS

1. There is nothing I can do to gain favor with God. I already have God's favor.
2. A belief in personal power is a form of exaltation which leads me to being humbled.
3. There is no personal power.
4. Humility is based on the spiritual truth that there is only one Presence and one Power—God.
4. The heart of a humble life is this: "It is no longer I who live, but Christ who lives in me."
5. The cycle of power is: I have the power. I am powerless. There is only one power, God, and It expresses Itself in me and through me.

AFFIRMATION
There is no such thing as personal power.

SUMMARY
The only true power is the power God is.

THE HUMILITY
OF PRAYER

PRAYER AS AN ACT OF WILL

Prayer is a call for humility, but we have made it our attempt to call on God to do our bidding. Prayer should be a supreme expression of humility, but we have made it an extension of our ego. Out of lack and self-will come our demands. We need a healing, a job, a relationship, peace of mind, to know what to do, etc. We have outlined what we want, often in great detail. In our infinite wisdom, we know the perfect solution, and only God can make it happen. We have prayed this way for thousands of years, and therefore we have prayed without humility.

We have followed Saul in trying to gain favor with the Almighty. By praying the right way, by having enough faith, Spirit will smile upon us and be compelled to grant our wish. There is probably no area of spirituality that has received more attention than prayer, and yet it is an area where we have missed the mark.

We have failed to realize that the heart of prayer is intent—why we pray. Prayer for the majority of us has been about our earthly life, getting what we need and want.

Prayer, in truth, is about our spiritual life and our relationship with God.

We are spiritual beings with capabilities beyond measure, but the expression of our true selves remains a potential when our focus is upon earthly needs. This is tragic in one sense, but it is also part of our spiritual journey and rite of passage into the realization of what it means to be made in the image and after the likeness of God. However, now our time has come to change our intent. The good news is that the universe has been devised in a way that allows our earthly experience to flow out of our ever deepening relationship with the Presence. God first, then the world. Jesus put it this way: "But seek first his kingdom . . . and all these things shall be yours as well" (Matthew 6:33).

PRAYER HUMBLES US

Who has not been humbled in prayer? We ask, and nothing happens. We wonder if there is a God or if there is, does God care about us and our life? I can assure you that there is a caring presence of Love that permeates the universe, but our self-will has built a barrier to the experience of this Presence. And so we are humbled. Even our prayers activate the principle, ". . . for every one who exalts himself will be humbled, but he who humbles himself will be exalted" (Luke 18:14).

From a humble position, we can see things differently. We can take the step of humbling ourselves. We begin by changing our intent.

Let us conduct an experiment. For the next forty days, let us ask in prayer for an experience of the Presence. For forty days, let us put aside our earthly needs and acknowledge that our greatest need is to know God. During this period of time, our prayers will follow a simple four step process. (It is outlined in greater detail in the 40 day guide included in this book.)

First, we acknowledge that there is a God. Secondly, we ask only to know and experience the Presence. Next, we wait expectantly in silence as if we are waiting for the arrival of a dear friend. And lastly, we are willing to act upon guidance that comes as the result of prayer. This is a humble process without self-will or an attempt to gain favor with Spirit. There is no assertion of personal power, no attempt to gain personal possessions. Underlying this fourfold process is the knowing that we are God's beloved and that the time has come to allow ourselves to be cleansed of what stands between us and a life of oneness with Spirit.

PRAYER HUMBLES US AGAIN

When we pray the simple prayer of waiting, it is easy to believe that we are doing it right. After all, our intent is pure. We think surely God will be compelled, but it does not happen because we have resurrected our sense of personal power. Like those who built the tower of Babel, we believe that through our prayer of waiting we can touch the Creator. An awareness of Spirit will dawn in us. This is not true.

Our souls are prepared through our actions, but the experience of the Presence comes through grace. It is like the farmer who prepares the field and plants the seed. He cannot make the plants grow and the harvest come. Other forces are at work. The rains must come and sun must shine. These come from above. They are grace.

THE HUMILITY OF WAITING

From this humble position, we once again let go of personal power and wait. It is during the waiting that another form of humility comes upon us. Many people quit the pursuit of prayer for one of two reasons. The first is that nothing seems to happen. This humbles us again, for we eventually realize that we are seeking something for ourselves.

This is a difficult habit to break because it has been our way for so many years. The good news is that we are close to a breakthrough, for the soul that truly seeks only God is worthy of being a friend of God.

The second reason prayer is difficult is that many people find they cannot sit quietly and expectantly because their minds wander. Please note that I said nothing about whether the mind was supposed to wander or not. The end result is we believe we have failed. The feeling of powerlessness has returned. We falsely believe we are not meant for prayer, stillness, and silence. Our excuse is that we are people of action. Waiting expectantly is not for us. This is a crucial moment. We have been humbled, and we have the opportunity to humble ourselves, but excuses are our attempt to lift ourselves up. This is not our work. Spirit will lift us up if humility finds a home in us.

Waiting is the most difficult part of the spiritual journey and the unfoldment of our prayer life. Waiting and the roving mind humble us again and again, but their blessing is that they quicken in us a need for persistence. They tell us about the true nature of our intent. They ask us if we really want a relationship with Spirit. Do we want to live as spiritual beings or as human beings?

WHEN GOD PRAYS

A strange idea came to me not long ago. For many years, I have thought of me praying, of humanity praying. This seems obvious because there are things I do as part of my prayer life. I have believed these practices to be prayer. Perhaps they are because the traditional belief is that prayer is something that the human family does. Then a strange, non-traditional thought came to me.

If I am asking for a relationship with Spirit, then answered prayer is actually an experience of the Presence.

And if there is nothing I can do to make this happen because it is an act of grace, then the experiences I have as a part of my spiritual life are things that God does. They are God praying.

This changed me. The importance in prayer shifted from what I am doing to what God is doing. The crucial point is will I observe and experience deeply what God is doing? This is the question.

For me, this is the ultimate in the humility of prayer. There are things that I do as a part of my prayer process. Most of them are centered upon intent. They are simply an expression of my soul's yearning for union with my Creator. They are natural and at their deepest level, they are love. This is my prayer. However, when the experience comes, when I catch a glimpse of truth, of reality, of the way it really is, it is not me who prays; it is God.

GOD IS ENOUGH

Humanity's prayers have lacked humility. We have been willful and desirous of all manner of earthly things. Now we know that God is enough. We can put aside our human needs and get in touch with our spiritual need to know and experience the Presence.

Our prayers have been laced with personal power. We have thought that through our efforts we could get the Almighty to do our bidding. Now we know the meaning of the words Paul received from God, "My grace is sufficient for you" (II Corinthians 12:9).

The experience we want most is an experience of the Presence and it comes as a gift, as an act of grace. It is an activity of Spirit rather than something we accomplish.

Admittedly, our prayers have focused on personal possession. Occasionally, we pray for others, but the majority of prayers prayed on the planet are for self. Now we know that nothing is ours aside from our consciousness. It is the only possession we carry with us through eternity, and the only part of our consciousness that endures is our awareness of God.

These are the barriers to the life we are meant to live: willfulness, personal power, and personal possession. They have no place in our life of prayer, for the purest prayer is an expression of humility; it is the touch of the divine.

Key Ideas

1. Prayer has been an act of self-will.
2. It is a false notion to think that if I pray the "right way or the right prayer" I will get what I want.
3. Intent is the most important part of prayer.
4. Prayer is about my spiritual life, not my earthly life.
5. My earthly life is destined to flow out of my relationship with God.
6. The humble prayer asks for an awareness of God.
7. The highest prayer is the one God prays.

Affirmation

I put aside my human needs and ask for an awareness of Spirit.

Summary

Prayer humbles me and frees me of willfulness and aspiring for personal power and personal possession.

CHAPTER FIVE

THE HUMILITY
OF MYSTERY

BECOME AS A CHILD

"The disciples came to Jesus, saying, 'Who is the greatest in the kingdom of heaven?' And calling to him a child, he put him in the midst of them, and said, 'Truly, I say to you, unless you turn and become like children, you will never enter the kingdom of heaven. Whoever humbles himself like this child, he is the greatest in the kingdom of heaven'" (Matthew 18:1-4).

Using a child as an example of humility is an interesting choice because a child often attempts to get his way and to discover and assert his personal power. It seems to be part of growing up. In addition, there are times when a child will cling to his possessions. Not only will he consider things his, he will refuse to share them with others.

We have all witnessed this in children, so why did Jesus use a child as an example of humility? What quality is he making apparent to the disciples? What is it that children have that we lack or once had and lost? The answer is awe and wonder.

For a child, everything is new. A toddler, for instance, probes and investigates the world by thrusting into his mouth everything that will fit. Perhaps this little one is try-ing to digest all he sees and touches. He is trying to make it a part of himself. Mystically, this spiritual being who cur-rently inhabits a small body instinctively knows that his world is a part of him, and he is in awe of it.

This understanding and approach to life is natural to us. There is no effort or rational process that causes us to act this way. We are children, and children embrace the unknown. They consider the mysterious a friend. The strange is some-thing to get to know. For children, life is an adventure, and by living spontaneously, they learn and grow. There are hurtful experiences like the pain that comes from touching a flame or hot item on the stove, but the burn does not usually dampen the child's sense of awe and wonder. In fact, learning experi-ences like the hot flame can increase the sense of awe and wonder. They want to know more and understand why.

Sadly, adults are usually different. We are willing to sac-rifice awe and wonder in order to be free of pain. We are willing to forego adventure in order to have security. For adults, the familiar is safe, but it is also stayed and stagnant. We fail to realize that people who follow their bliss are the most secure people on earth.

THE ROOT OF HUMILITY

We grow up and apparently because of our increased height we are farther from one of the roots of humility—mystery. Wonder and mystery go together, and when we try to live in a world without mystery, we live in a world with-out wonder. This is a great tragedy, for we no longer seek out the unknown. We are no longer explorers like we were as children. We flee to the known world, for this is where we believe we will find security.

In our attempt to avoid pain and find security we cast out awe and wonder. Mystery is no longer a friend; it is a foe. We no longer see the beauty around us. The sky is filled with color, yet our minds are dark. Roads which lead to purpose and joy are not taken. We take the known path and think all is well, but even straight roads fade into the distance. We may think we know where they lead, but we do not. Unexpected adventures are along the way if we will allow ourselves to experience them. In fact, life that seems so clear turns out to be a sinuous road with hills and valleys that make it impossible to look around the bend. This was a lesson I had to learn. It was humbling and therefore uncomfortable, but the gift was that I discovered that humility and mystery are companions for the journey.

Years ago I had a spiritual experience that helped me through a difficult time. For years, I had sensed a greater good in my life and wanted to know what it was. I continually tried to look around the bend in the road to determine what was ahead. Unfortunately, this forward look was destroying my present moment. There was much to enjoy in my current situation, but I was not happy. My wife often asked me why I was not content. Many people, Nancy pointed out, would love to live the life I was living, but not me.

Finally in a time of prayer, the answer came. Spirit said to me, "Unless mystery is a part of your life, I am not a part of your life, for I am mystery." This experience transformed me. I discovered that mystery did not mean insecurity; it meant that I was not alone, that Spirit was with me.

If mystery is a part of your life and you are in the midst of some situation you do not comprehend, do not be concerned. Become like a child, embrace the mystery and walk into the unknown humble and willing to be led. As you do so, you will discover that a mighty Presence is with you. As you embrace the unknown, you will find everlasting arms around you. As you take your first unsteady steps into tomorrow, you will sense spiritual forces gathering in you.

I now believe that the most accurate description of God is mystery. The Bible says that God is Love and that God is Spirit, but aren't both of these mysterious? Who, for instance, understands love? And who truly knows the nature of Spirit?

The point is this: the truly humble do not know what is best for themselves or others. They understand that there will always be mystery, for life is hopefully the result of the touch of the divine. These fortunate ones know that mystery is the womb where faith is born.

Faith is not knowing what is going to happen. Faith is knowing that no matter what happens, we are one with God. Faith is not a way to control our lives. Faith does not need to look into the future; it walks into each moment hand in hand with Spirit. One thing is certain; we never walk alone.

The humble person knows it is not necessary or possible to comprehend the nuances of life. This is why humility and mystery are companions for life's journey. When we lack humility, we try to control our lives because we believe we know what is best. The humble one surrenders to mystery and finds contentment while resting in God's everlasting arms. This is where there is security, in mystical oneness with the Presence. The wonder is that a consciousness of God is manifesting itself in and as our lives. This produces mystery, for who can predict how a consciousness of the Presence will make itself known in the world? However, rest assured that it will show itself in ways that are beyond our dreams and human aspirations.

LETTING GOALS BE SET

This is why we must be careful in setting goals. Often the practices associated with this way of life are an attempt to control, and therefore lack humility. In addition, many of our goals flow from a consciousness of lack. In other words, we look at what we do not have and create a goal to fill the void. The weakness of this method is that the origin of our actions and endeavors is an empty cup. There is another way.

I recommend that you do not set goals, but that you let goals be set. This may seem to be a play on words, but I assure you it is not, for in this approach to living the beginning of action is an overflowing cup. We put God first and open ourselves to an experience of the Presence. Guidance and actions begin with God rather than something we do not have. This way of life is not control; it is surrender. This is not lack, it is fullness. We are guided to do a certain thing or pursue a particular endeavor, and so we act.

HUMBLE LIKE A CHILD

Jesus said that we must become like children in order to enter the kingdom of heaven. Could there be anything more mysterious than the kingdom? We know it to be within us, and we know it grows like a mustard seed. The Master also said it is at hand, it is here, and yet it is coming. What could this kingdom be? The answer is a consciousness of the Presence. Our awareness of God is within us. Our relationship with Spirit is ever growing. It is here now, but hopefully it will be even more on a future day as our consciousness of Spirit grows and spreads throughout our lives.

And yet what is more mysterious than our Creator? How will we ever enter into the mysterious kingdom of God if we are not willing to embrace the mystery that life on earth presents to us? Let us become like children and admit that we do not know. In the past, we have tried to control our lives; now let's simply live. Once we planned our lives day by day; now let us be like children and live moment by moment. Life lived this way is filled with mystery. It humbles us, but then we are lifted up by Spirit in the same way that Jesus exalted the child who stood in the midst of the disciples.

KEY IDEAS

1. Mystery is my friend.
2. Mystery humbles me.
3. My security is in my relationship with God.
4. Unless mystery is a part of my life, God is not a part of my life, for God is mystery.
5. Faith is not knowing what is going to happen. Faith is knowing that no matter what happens, I am one with God.
6. There is no peace and contentment in control.
7. I let goals be set.

AFFIRMATION

My life is filled with mystery, therefore my life is filled with God.

SUMMARY

I let what I do not know or understand humble me.

CHAPTER SIX

THE BEGINNING OF EXALTATION

THE GIFT OF HUMILITY

It is best to be humble, but exalting ourselves is not as bad as it seems. Remember that the humility principle assures us that whenever we exalt ourselves we will be humbled. An attempt to assert personal power, claim a deed as ours, or take the place of honor activates the principle. It may take awhile, but if we continue to live out of this same state of human consciousness, the day will come when we are humbled. Then we have a choice. We can maintain our belief in personal power or take a small step that leads to humility and then conscious oneness with God.

I recall reading one of my son's second grade papers. The assignment must have been to share something significant that happened to the students over the summer vacation. I was shocked to learn that Ben indicated his displeasure in discovering that he could not fly. It stirred me to realize that one of his secret summer projects was to learn to fly. (Thank God he did not try to leap off the roof of our house.) I also felt a degree of his disappointment. A learning experience such as trying to fly and discovering that we cannot join the birds in the sky can create a sense of limitation, or it can give us the gift of humility.

I wonder how many of us experience defeat and then take on a sense of limitation and failure rather than humility. In watching Ben grow up, I don't believe he chose a feeling of limitation. He chose humility and experienced a sense of wonder as he learned to appreciate God's wisdom in creating creatures that can fly.

Any defeat will humble us. This is part of the human condition. Once we experience a sense of failure, the crucial step is the next one. Will we carry a feeling of failure or will we take the next step and humble ourselves? The choice is ours, and it will determine whether we ultimately express more or less of what we truly are. The issue is this: all of us are humbled from time to time, but will we take the next step and humble ourselves?

COMING HOME

The story of the prodigal son is an example of both dimensions of the humility principle, ". . . for everyone who exalts himself will be humbled, but he who humbles himself will be exalted" (Luke 18:14). In this parable of Jesus', a man's son asks for his inheritance. His request is granted, and the son leaves his home and travels to a far country where he squanders his property in loose living.

The prodigal had a sense of personal possession. He wanted what was *his,* and the father gave according to the son's belief. It becomes obvious later in the story that the father is God and that the son is each of us.

What personal possession can we have that is not the Father's? The answer is given in the twenty-fourth psalm, "The earth is the Lord's and the fullness thereof, the world and those who dwell therein . . ." (Psalm 24:1). What worldly possession can we have that is ours eternally? Just as we have seen, there is no such thing as personal power and personal accomplishment because God is the only power; now we discover there is no such thing as personal possession. Instead, Spirit has given us the bounty of the earth to use and to share, but it is not ours. We have no claim to the things of the earth, for we are beings of Spirit.

The young man discovers this when a famine occurs in the far country where he has made his home. Actually, his soul or inner life is barren, and his sense of personal possession results in him being humbled. The man who is Jewish finds himself feeding swine (pigs were considered unclean in the Hebrew culture), and realizes that his sense of lack is so great that he is willing to eat the pods that have been given to the pigs. Luke 15:17-18 reveals what happens next. "But when he came to himself he said, 'How many of my Father's hired servants have bread enough and to spare, but I perish here with hunger! I will arise and go to my father . . .'"

The young man's realization while feeding the swine causes him to acknowledge his powerlessness and inability to solve his problem or lift himself up. This is an important awareness if he is to find his way home. This is also an important insight for us, for the prodigal's journey is often our own. It is vital that we come to ourselves just as the young son did. The self awareness may be hurtful emotionally, but in the midst of the hurt is humility. This is the one step that needs to be taken if we are to be lifted up. By coming to ourselves, we are homeward bound.

A powerful verse in the fifteenth chapter of Luke reveals another step to be taken when we feel powerless. It is the simple step that moves us from being humbled to humbling ourselves and ultimately to being lifted up by God. "And he arose and came to his father. But while he was yet at a distance, his father saw him and had compassion, and ran and embraced him and kissed him" (Luke 15: 20). The verse clearly indicates that by turning Godward, the Presence is revealed to us. For the person committed to living the humble life, a question naturally follows. How do I turn Godward? I have been trying to make contact with Spirit for quite some time. What do I do?

The answer is so simple, it is hardly believable to the human mind. Become prayerful and still and simply ask God, "Are You with me?" This human cry opens our souls and humbles us because it acknowledges that we feel alone and that we have reached that point in our spiritual unfoldment where only God can comfort our souls. From this simple question, we will come to hear three messages God speaks to every human being who seeks the mystical oneness. God's answer will declare three truths:

I am with you always.
You are my beloved.
I do not condemn you.

You may never actually hear these specific words, but in ways that only Spirit can convey, you will experience these three great truths. You will be lifted to the height of God's presence.

Here is another great truth. An awareness of God is exaltation. Our humanness may insist that exaltation is worldly fame, power, possessions, or adoration, but there is no height to such things. God's presence is the gift received when we come home and allow God to lift us up. And this gift is enough.

KEY IDEAS

1. A belief in personal possession is a form of human exaltation that leads to being humbled.
2. Once I have been humbled, the next step is for me to humble myself.
3. The beginning of humbling myself is to acknowledge my powerlessness.
4. The beginning of exaltation is to turn Godward.
5. I turn to my Father by simply asking, "Are You with me?" The answer is in three messages God reveals to every receptive human being.

   I am with you always.
   You are my beloved.
   I do not condemn you.
6. An awareness of God is exaltation.

AFFIRMATION

The earth is the Lord's and the fullness thereof . . .

SUMMARY

There is no such thing as personal possession.

CHAPTER SEVEN

THE HUMILITY OF FORGIVENESS

HAVING TO BE RIGHT

We have spiritual tendencies, but they are often overshadowed by our human inclinations. For instance, everyone wants to be right. No one wants to be wrong or to make mistakes. Our human tendency is to make mistakes, but not admit them. This makes humility difficult.

Our spiritual tendency is to love, and love makes forgiveness unnecessary, but when we resent another person regardless of the reason, forgiveness is required. Without it, we fail to express our spiritual nature. Love remains an imprisoned splendor even though its destiny is to freely give itself to the world.

As human beings, we have many challenges, but forgiveness is the most difficult and far-reaching, for it promotes peace in our lives and peace on earth. Not only do individuals withhold love from one another, they strike out and inflict pain, and consequently never discover who they really are. This is the root of conflict between races, cultures, and nations. We refuse to be humble because we feel the need to be right. This is a great problem, because right is a form of exaltation. Right may fortify us for a time, but eventually it will humble us and present us with the opportunity to forgive and to love again.

NO FORGIVENESS WITHOUT HUMILITY

There is no forgiveness without humility. When we are humble we have let go of being right; we have let go of our pain and our need for revenge. In fact, expressing our spiritual nature has become more important than the other person seeing it our way or being punished.

Forgiveness is for us, not the other person. This was illustrated by Jesus when he answered Peter's question, ". . . Lord, how often shall my brother sin against me, and I forgive him? As many as seven times? Jesus said to him, 'I do not say to you seven times, but seventy times seven'" (Matthew 18:21-22). Imagine a situation where a person keeps behaving in a fashion that requires him to be forgiven over one hundred times. Obviously, forgiveness is having no effect on this person. However, Jesus is telling us that forgiveness is vital to our own well-being. Being right is no longer the issue. Our spiritual unfoldment is at stake, and the question is will we express our loving nature.

The truth is we all make mistakes. This was Jesus' message to the men who wanted to stone the woman caught in adultery. "Let him who is without sin among you be the first to throw a stone at her." This was his message in the Sermon on the Mount when he said, "Why do you see the speck that is in your brother's eye, but do not notice the log that is in your own eye? Or how can you say to your brother, 'Let me take the speck out of your eye,' when there is the log in your own eye? You hypocrite, first take the log out of your own eye, and then you shall see clearly to take the speck out of your brother's eye" (Matthew 7:3-5). These verses humble us, and from our humble position we will never actually try to take the speck from another's eye. As we shall see later in this chapter, we will simply accept our brother as he is, and in this way love him unconditionally.

FORGIVENESS IS A RETURN TO LOVE

Forgiveness is a return to love. It is an expression of our loving nature. What makes it forgiveness is that there was resentment, now there is love. We had refused to humble ourselves, but now we make ourselves small. We see this in the story of the woman who washed Jesus' feet with her tears and anointed them with oil. Luke 7:36-50 tells us that the Master was at a Pharisee's house. The religious leader has followed none of the usual customs upon Jesus' entry into the home. However, a woman has entered who is most likely a prostitute. In the scripture, she is called a sinner. The woman is crying and wetting Jesus' feet with her tears and drying them with her hair. The woman has much to feel guilty about, but she is humbling herself before Jesus and the others present.

While this is taking place, the Pharisee is thinking that if Jesus was really a prophet of God he would never allow this woman to touch him. Jesus knows the man's thoughts and tells him a story that teaches him a lesson, but then he turns to the woman and says to the religious leader, "Do you see this woman? I entered your house, you gave me no water for my feet, but she has wet my feet with her tears and wiped them with her hair . . . I tell you, her sins, which are many, are forgiven, for she loved much . . ." (Luke 7:44, 47).

Two ideals are evident in this story: humility and love. The woman humbled herself, and it moved her to tears, but she did not run from her feelings. She let her humility call forth love from the heart of God within her. And she was forgiven. This is our path, and we must walk it. We are to humble ourselves and love much.

Our first steps are usually painful because we have made a habit of holding on to our negativity and holding in the goodness of God. Now it begins to rise from our souls. Often there is a rush of emotion. How else could it be? Exalting ourselves causes discomfort, and divine love overwhelms us.

THE FIRST STEP

The first step is to humble ourselves. This can take many forms. For instance, I have found myself in situations where people question my motivation or integrity. In the past, I have immediately denied this and begun to build my defenses. My mind closed, and I could not even entertain the possibility that the person might be correct. Through experience (this means painful experiences), I have learned to assume for a time that the person is accurate. Perhaps he has perceived something to which I am blind. This technique opens my mind. It allows me to genuinely see another person's viewpoint. Quite frankly, this is a humbling process, but it is helpful. I have found it a genuine way to truthfully look at myself.

I am sorry are three powerful words. *Please forgive me* are equally powerful. This is the humility of forgiveness. I remember a television program many years ago called *Happy Days*. One of the main characters was Fonzie. He was a maverick with a good heart. When he made a mistake, he would try to apologize. However, he could hardly say the word sorry. He would stammer and begin again and again. The point is it is difficult to say I am sorry. This is true even when we are mistaken. Imagine what it would be like to be falsely accused of something and never defend yourself.

Long ago I heard a story of a priest who was falsely accused of fathering a child. There was much outrage in the community. The priest was innocent, but he never stated that he was. Instead, he endured the scorn of those around him and helped care for and raise the child. Imagine the impact on the young mother who knew the priest was not the father of the child.

In later years when the priest was asked why he chose to help the young woman and her child even though he was falsely accused of being the father, the priest said that the false accusation was a cry for help, and he simply responded.

The humility of forgiveness has many faces. We can apologize when we have made a mistake and when we have not. Each is a form of humility that frees our souls and leads us to love.

WHEN WE ARE WRONGED

When we are wronged, there is a reason. We may never know why, but one thing we can be assured of is that we have the opportunity to grow in love. Usually we struggle to forgive when we are wronged. We are actually struggling to grow and to love again. It is time to grow into another person who has never endured the difficult situation.

This was the insight of my wife Nancy when she grew through a difficult and hurtful situation. She struggled for years to be free from negative feelings and memories. Finally, the breakthrough occurred. She had a revelation that she was no longer the person who had experienced the hurtful event. She might look similar to that person, but on the inside, she was different. Who she was today had never experienced the event of the past. This revelation from God healed her. This is what happens when we humble ourselves and refuse to give in to hurt and resentment. A form of exaltation comes, an experience of the Presence, granting us new insight and making us a new creation.

NO SPECK IN MY BROTHER'S EYE

Forgiveness is for us; the work is to remove the log from our own eye. Jesus said when this task was complete, we would be able to remove the speck from our brother's eye. I am convinced that Jesus knew that once we truly practiced forgiveness we would no longer feel the need to remove the speck from our brother's eye. In fact, if we looked carefully, we would probably notice that the speck was gone.

This is because forgiveness is a return to love, and love never demands that another person change. A loving individual accepts others the way they are, and therefore creates an atmosphere that invites the other person's transformation.

This is a call for humility because it requires that we let go of being right, having others conform to our standards of conduct, or doing what we want them to do. Righteous indignation is no longer justified. We no longer pursue who is right. We pursue personal transformation. Those who have undergone this change discover that it is no longer important to change others. All that matters is that we remain in love. But if we leave love's side, we know the path that comes full circle and returns to love passes through a place called humility.

Key Ideas

1. Forgiveness is for me, not the other person.
2. Forgiveness is a return to love.
3. Forgiveness requires humility.
4. I refuse to be humble because I feel the need to be right.
5. Right is a form of exaltation.
6. Love never demands that another person change.

Affirmation

I don't need to be right. I need to forgive.

Summary

Nothing and no one can stop me from expressing my true nature.

CHAPTER EIGHT

THE EGO TRAP

THE TRAP IS SET

George Lamsa was a scholar well known in the Bible community. He had an extensive understanding of Aramaic, the language Jesus spoke, and translated the scripture from the ancient, eastern Aramaic texts. His talents and accolades were many. Often when he was introduced, his accomplishments were carefully outlined. In typical eastern fashion, he would begin his speech by saying, "I am a humble man."

Perhaps Mr. Lamsa knew about the ego trap. Jesus set this trap for his disciples and for us. The twentieth chapter of Matthew records a time when disciples James and John, the sons of Zebedee, declared their desire to sit at Jesus' right and left hand in his kingdom. They were thinking as did many people of this era that a messiah, whom they believed to be Jesus, was going to establish an earthly kingdom. The two disciples wanted positions of authority in this state established and governed by the son of God.

The simple man of Nazareth answered, "You know that the rulers of the Gentiles lord it over them, and their great men exercise authority over them. It shall not be so among you; but whoever would be great among you must be your servant . . ." (Matthew 20:25-26). This verse sets the ego trap. The promise is that greatness follows the one who is a servant to others. Imagine the disciples trying to achieve greatness through service. Their motivation would be self-centered, but their behavior would be exemplary.

The gentleness of Jesus is evident in this conversation with his disciples. He did not admonish them for aspiring to greatness. He led them to humility. Jesus understood that even though the disciples' initial motivation was selfish that they would eventually experience joy and humility because the desire to serve would become the driving force of their lives. Their need for greatness and authority would fall away. In their place would be humility and a genuine concern for other people.

Often there are programs in the judicial system that require youthful offenders to serve others. A few hours helping a handicapped child and experiencing the joy of serving can cause a change of heart in a young person who still longs for a meaningful life. Obviously, the goal in these programs is not punishment; it is transformation. The young men and women have the opportunity to discover that they can have a positive effect on another person's life. They can discover that their sense of worth is enhanced not by thinking of themselves, but by thinking of another. This is often enough to turn a life destined for crime into one that is dedicated to the common good.

Jesus did not just talk about being the servant, he demonstrated the servant consciousness by washing the feet of his disciples. They viewed Jesus as the Master. They were present when he walked on the water. They witnessed the lame walking. They saw the blind see. Imagine the impact of their Master washing their feet. Cosmic forces moved through him, but he chose to render service to them. Peter, for example, initially refused to have his feet washed.

Undoubtedly, the disciples were puzzled, but Jesus' humble act made him greater in their eyes. In the years to come, they would follow his example. They would eventually see that Jesus was doing more than washing their feet. He was trying to cleanse their souls of the pursuit of greatness and put in its place a longing for the humble life.

THE TRAP IS SPRUNG

We, too, must face the ego trap. We draw near to it when we first believe we have the power of accomplishment. We take a step closer and are lured into the trap when we succeed and believe we are the source of the success. Greatness is close at hand, or so we think.

The trap is sprung, and we are caught in it when we discover the possibility of being held in high esteem in the eyes of others. This, we discern, comes through service, so we forge ahead supposedly serving others while actually being motivated to serve ourselves. We can delude ourselves for years, but it is also possible for us to break through into the humble life.

On this day, we experience not greatness but a great joy. We have lost our ego self and found our true self because we gave attention to another person. We served without thought of return, and love emerged from within us, transforming us forever. Our ego thought it was bound for greatness, but our humble self was eventually released in the world because it was bound for service.

We succeed best when our esteem is rooted in our relationship with Spirit rather than the words and compliments of other people. At first we say we want to serve others, but the truth is we want to be served. We may help members of our human family, but we are actually trying to elicit praise from them. This is the greatness we seek, and it will never fulfill our souls. Fulfillment comes from the joy we experience in service. The characteristic of a person caught in the ego trap is twofold. First, he must have more and more praise, and secondly when disapproval is given, he is devastated. He is humbled, and the humility principle once more presents him with a new beginning.

Now we can choose again. We can fake service to others and try to have them call us great, or we can examine our motivation. Why do we try to help others? This takes brutal honesty, but it is worth it. We become more genuine and honest with other people, and more honest with ourselves. For the first time in our lives, we have personal integrity.

COMING FULL CIRCLE

The ego trap can be avoided, but it is a path many of us choose to walk. It is a valley way, but with self-examination and continued commitment to service, we find the humble life. Nothing invites the touch of the Divine as much as service to others. It is self forgetting at its best.

When I was first a minister, I went to visit a convicted murderer who was serving a life sentence in prison. I listened intently to what he was willing to share that day. When I rose to leave, he placed his hand on the glass that separated us, and I did the same. It was a simple gesture, but one symbolic of the spiritual oneness we had shared. I felt the Presence that day, and I am convinced that it was because of self forgetting. For a brief time, there was no Jim; there was only a man, a spiritual being, who had once forgotten that he was made in God's image.

We can move beyond the ego trap if we are aware of why we do the things we do. Life is not to be lived blindly. Motivation and intent determine the direction of our lives and the events that come to us. Some of us are in service oriented jobs. However, all of us, even the unemployed or retired, have opportunities to serve. In congested traffic, we can let a waiting motorist enter in front of us. We can interact pleasantly with the agent to whom we report our lost luggage.

If we fail to respond to these opportunities, we are not yet worthy of the humble life. If we do respond, it is good to ask why. This simple question brings us full circle to the beginning where we can discover a pure intent or one that is tainted with self. If we find ourselves in the ego trap, we can easily escape by putting ourselves aside. Our best ally is our attention. When we give the gift of our attention to another individual, a service consciousness is born in us just as it was in Jesus when he washed the feet of his disciples. This enables us to feel the gentle touch of the Divine. However, when we focus on ourselves we are unable to feel the Divine touch even though we are washing the feet of another. Only a pure intent to serve creates a sensitivity in our souls that allows us to sense the Presence and to live the humble life.

KEY IDEAS

1. Selfless service is an act of humility and the sustainer of the humble life.
2. Greatness is not a worthy motivation for a spiritual being.
3. It is important that I ask myself why I want to serve.
4. A true life of service is a life of humility.

AFFIRMATION
I live in service to Spirit and Its creation.

SUMMARY
I live not to be served, but to serve.

CHAPTER NINE

HUMILITY'S COMPANION

ANOTHER PARADOX

The earth belongs to the meek. To most people this is nonsense because everyone knows that the earth belongs to the strong and aggressive. Only the fittest survive. It was this way when only animals inhabited the earth, and now that humans dominate the landscape, this rule remains. When we judge by appearances, this is the world we see. We honor strength that makes its own way and aggressiveness that cares little for the weak. We are blind to a higher law that is at work. Like the humility principle, this law is a paradox. "Blessed are the meek, for they shall inherit the earth" (Matthew 5:5).

This beatitude seems as far-fetched as the idea that humility is the key that unleashes spiritual forces from within us, and yet we have seen this is true. Meekness is a worthy companion for humility, for together they enable us to live a life of oneness with God. In fact, they promise such a life. Without these two, humility and meekness, conscious oneness with the One is not possible, and our earthly experience is stress and fatigue.

There is great power in meekness, for it is the open door through which the Presence blesses our lives. It is through meekness that a harmonious life of joy comes to us. We live effortlessly, and what comes to us comes as an inheritance. Inherit is a key word in the beatitude, for when something is received in this way, it is not because of what we have done, but because of our heritage or roots. When something is inherited, it is because of who we are, not what we do or how strong and aggressive we are. Inheritance is God's way, and it is the best way for something to come into being.

However, this way of life requires responsibility. We are God's creation, and we are made in the image and after the likeness of our Creator. The inheritance comes when we know who and what we are. This is not an intellectual thing. A spiritual revelation is required. We must experience our sacred self. Then out of this consciousness our world is formed. It is inherited.

JESUS BEFORE PILATE

Jesus standing before Pilate is the supreme example of meekness and humility. Rome's procurator believes himself powerful, for the imperial might of Caesar stands behind him. Roman legions have conquered the known world and are supposedly the sole power in the empire. Jewish zealots stand prepared to fight against Rome and to rid Israel of the Roman curse, but even these freedom fighters acknowledge that Rome is a formidable foe with which to reckon. These are the accepted facts, but they are not the truth. Jesus knows the truth, and it frees him to speak boldly. "You would have no power over me unless it had been given you from above . . ." (John 19:11). This prisoner is telling Pilate that he stands before him not because of Pilate's power, but because his presence in the praetorium is part of a divine plan. The power is from above.

Jesus does not resist Pilate because he sees nothing to resist. God is the only Power in his life and in his universe. He is meek, not because there is nothing he can do or because of fear, but because he understands that his life flows from an awareness of God.

LIFE IS A CONSCIOUSNESS OF GOD

Jesus stood before Pilate, but he lived and breathed the presence of God. This was his source of peace and strength, and it allowed him to be meek.

The meek know true power. They understand that our thoughts, feelings, and beliefs manifest themselves as our life experience. No matter how hard we try or how long we persist, unless a consciousness exists within us for a certain happening, it will not come to pass. Some people interpret this idea to mean that we should envision or think about specific occurrences until they become a part of our inner-most thoughts and beliefs. Then they will come into being. This method is helpful and part of our rite of passage in spiritual unfoldment, but eventually a spiritual insight causes us to cease this way of living.

We realize that life as it is meant to be is a consciousness of God. Unless we are awake to the Presence, we are not fully alive. When this revelation dawns in us, it changes us forever. We no longer try to create a consciousness of things, events, and happenings we deem important. We let go of trying to direct the course of our life and give our attention to knowing and experiencing Spirit. We believe an awareness of God is destined to give birth to our experience. Who is so wise as to know how a divine consciousness will manifest itself? No one can determine this in advance, so our souls are filled with awe and wonder.

We are meek because God is our strength and because a consciousness of Spirit is constantly giving birth to our life. Jesus stood peacefully before Pilate because he knew the one Presence and one Power was at work. He bowed his head, and his Father raised him up. Pilate gave the order for

Jesus to be lifted up and placed on a cross, but the Presence lifted Jesus above all pain and human strife.

GOD IS MEEK

We express our true selves when we are meek because God is meek. There is thunder in the sky and great strength in the wind and the wave, but God is meek with us. The Power of the universe does not push Itself upon us. The only Presence and Power is humble. It waits meekly for us to seek It.

The humble life is a life of inheritance, but before we receive the inheritance, we must discover who we are. When we know our spiritual nature, we experience the outer world and enjoy its fruits without making them the object and focus of our existence. For instance, healing is experienced through meekness. Jobs are obtained, and deep, enduring friendships are formed through meekness. Think of the best that life can be and know it can be inherited. We have only to be meek.

KEY IDEAS

1. I inherit my world, not because of what I do or because of personal power, but because of who I am.
2. To inherit is to discover who I am.
3. Life is a consciousness of God.
4. Because God is the only Presence and only Power, true consciousness is of God.
5. Because God is my strength, I am meek.

AFFIRMATION

I am meek because my life flows from an awareness of the Presence.

SUMMARY

I inherit my world because I am meek.

54

CHAPTER TEN

AN INVITATION TO THE HUMBLE LIFE

MANY PATHS

The humble life awaits us. It is part of Spirit's plan for Its creation. We begin life in seeming weakness because we can do little for ourselves. We cannot walk or lift the lightest object. The simplest task appears beyond us. Then we begin to discover our capabilities and acquire toys we call our own. We learn about personal possessions.

Our sense of power increases, and we are able to perform tasks that bring us praise and feelings of joy. We conclude we are competent and worthy of success and even greater accomplishments. We learn of personal power, but there seems to be deeds we cannot do. We try harder and recommit ourselves to using our talents to the fullest, but still some things remain just beyond our grasp.

We are now prepared for the humble life. We are standing on the threshold of understanding the nature of true power. And this is not because of what we have accomplished, but because of what we have failed to accomplish.

Other people take another path to the humble life. These individuals may never feel a sense of power or accomplishment. In fact, the life they live may leave them with a deep sense of powerlessness. It is from this humble state that a step can be taken that will open the soul to humility. This step occurs when the soul turns Godward. This person will soon discover that when God is his desire, the bounty of the earth is also his. All that is needed for life here is received, and it comes effortlessly.

Another group of people takes a different and, in many ways, a more difficult route to a life of oneness with God. They, too, feel a sense of powerlessness, but they attempt to hide it from others and from themselves. These individuals try to exalt themselves in an attempt to cast aside their feelings of powerlessness. Their ego strength is great, and they may seem to accomplish much. These people activate the law of humility, ". . . for every one who exalts himself will be humbled, but he who humbles himself will be exalted" (Luke 18:14). For them, life can be a series of highs and lows, like a roller coaster ride—up and down, up and down. They exalt themselves and are humbled. Then they humble themselves and are exalted.

HUMILITY—A CALL TO POWER

Humility allows the power and presence that is God to be expressed. Jesus spoke from experience when he said, "My Father is working still, and I am working" (John 5:17). This is partnership. We have our work to do, but first and foremost we allow Spirit to move in and through and as our lives.

There are a number of things we can do that prepare us for the humble life. These activities help us see God at work on earth and in our lives.

1. We can consider the wonder of the universe. Like Ben, we can attempt to fly, and discover humility. Sitting for even a brief time while we observe nature

at work will help us discover how little we know. This is awe, the beginning of humility.

2. We can consider our mistakes. There is no need to dwell upon them, but the errors we make are evident. Exaltation begins when we are mature and humble enough to admit our mistakes to ourselves and to another person. This is a core idea of the spiritual program of Alcoholics Anonymous. Each person undergoing recovery conducts a fearless moral inventory of himself or herself. Then the discoveries are shared with a trusted confidant. The result is that the person experiences the acceptance of another individual even though this person knows his darkest secrets. Needless to say, this is humbling, but it is an important step toward self-acceptance.

3. We can assume the role of servant by helping others. Humility and happiness do not come when we are the center of our universe. Simply focusing fully upon another person and their needs will in a strange way help to meet one of our deep soul needs—the need to make a difference. This is God's work, and it is accomplished when we are willing to give the gift of our attention to another member of the human family.

4. We can let a powerful idea be the focus of our prayer life for a period of 40 days. *I of myself can do nothing, through Spirit I can do all things.* Memorizing this statement or speaking it often will not transform our lives. However, if we rest with these words and allow the Presence to reveal their inner meaning, the humble life is near.

TOUCH OF THE DIVINE

Although the activities outlined above and throughout this book are helpful, it is important to understand that humility is not achieved. It is not an accomplishment. There is no formula to follow that will bring about the desired result. Humility is a gift, an activity of grace, a revelation to the soul that God is the only power. When we receive this gift, our work is God's work. In the past, our sense of personal power built its little castles, but they were made of sand and the movement of the tides washed them away. What is done in humility endures.

Humility allows us to live and find comfort in the mystery of life. We feel no need to make life happen. Instead, we inherit our experiences. They flow from a consciousness of the Presence, and who is so wise to know how the Mind that conceived the universe will shape our life?

Humility is a gift of God that lifts us up, but exaltation cannot occupy even a corner of our minds unless we understand exaltation to be an awareness of God. We can try to be humble, but humility comes with the touch of the Divine. We can let go of control, willfulness, personal power and possession and give attention to others, but we are humble only when God comes alive in us.

One day, when we believe ourselves to be powerless or when we forget ourselves, the hand of God will touch us. In that moment we will enter a larger world—one in which it is not we who live, but God who lives as us. This is the promise of the humble life.

A Forty Day Guide to
the Transcendent Life

The ideas shared in *The Transcendent Life* are meant to be lived. Reading and learning about the humble life is not enough. Spirit is not fully alive in the intellect. The full expression of the Presence includes the heart and the activities of daily living. This is why *A Forty Day Guide to the Transcendent Life was written,* to help you develop the consciousness that invites the touch of the Divine.

Do not feel compelled to complete this section of the book in 40 days. Forty days represents the time required to complete a task. You may want to spend more than a day working with some of the ideas or activities presented. Take as much time as you need. The humble life is special. It cannot be rushed or made to happen. May the next forty days be the most sacred days you have ever lived.

DAY ONE

Humility is the pathway to the life I want to live.

1 For quite some time, I have assumed that life could be more than it currently is. In fact, I have tried to make it more, to make it happen, but to no avail. I have searched for the path that leads to a creative, compassionate, and highly productive life. Even though I believed this life to be my destiny, I wondered if it would ever come to be.

Now I sense that it is near because I have found the path I am to walk. The byway is alluring and seems so right, but I sense it is not an easy journey even though there is a promise of effortlessness. Today, I must decide if I am willing to walk this path. Am I willing to have my mind, heart, and actions united in the pursuit of humility?

Many people know the location of Mount Everest. The path to the summit has been trod by many through the years, but not everyone chooses to climb the arduous trail to the summit. So it is with the way of humility. I have the opportunity to live as I have never lived before. Am I willing to take the first step?

In the space below, write a statement that expresses your willingness to walk the path that leads to the humble life.

....

....

....

....

....

....

....

....

D A Y   T W O

Effortlessness is evidence of humility.

2 Through the years, I have worked hard. At times the fruits of my labor were evident and could be enjoyed. At others times I asked, "What am I doing? Why am I doing this? What's the use?" I wished it could be different. I sensed it could be different, but how? There were times when tasks were effortlessly accomplished. Could it be that I caught a glimpse of how I was to live and work? This seems to be the promise of humility. Could it be true?

I have heard about a state of consciousness in which work is done without taking thought. Athletes sometimes refer to this state. In fact, the most successful athletes of all time owe their extraordinary feats to this effortless state of mind and heart. They receive credit for the performance, but they know forces that transcend them are at work.

The effortless life is not reserved for the athletically gifted. Effortlessness is evidence of humility, and therefore it can be experienced in all areas of human endeavor. As I give myself to the humble life, I remain vigilant and open to the experience of effortlessness.

My commitment is not to work so hard. I will do my part, but I will also leave room for Spirit to do Its work, for I suspect work is done effortlessly when God is my yokefellow.

TODAY MEDITATE UPON MATTHEW 11:28-30.

Within these verses is a key to effortlessness.

"Come to me, all who labor and are heavy laden,
and I will give you rest. Take my yoke upon you, and learn from me;
for I am gentle and lowly in heart, and you will find rest for your souls.
For my yoke is easy, and my burden is light."

DAY THREE

Effort is prelude to the effortless life.

To work effortlessly would be a dream come true, but I am finding that effort is prelude to the effortless life. It is this way when I am yoked to Spirit. The verses of scripture from the previous day refer to a common event of Jesus' time. A family might have only one oxen, donkey, or beast of burden. When it came time to plow the field, one of the family members would be yoked to the animal. The oxen would carry most of the burden, but it was necessary for the person to hold up his side of the yoke so the plowing could be completed.

There is work for me to do, and I am willing to do it. I do not walk the path of humility looking for a life of ease. I want to live in unity with Spirit.

Today think of yourself as yoked to Spirit.
What one thing are you willing to do that will contribute to
God's work and to your discovery of the humble life?

DAY FOUR

The humility principle is active in my life.

4 The Creator in Its wisdom has conceived principles that govern my life and the lives of everyone. One law of life I have recently discovered is the humility principle. ". . . for everyone who exalts himself will be humbled, but he who humbles himself will be exalted" (Luke 18:14). This is not a law with which I can choose to interact. It is a principle, and therefore it is always active in my life. Either I humble myself, and I am exalted, or I exalt myself, and I am humbled.

I cannot decide to put this principle aside until I am ready to work with it. It is always working with me. However, I have a choice to make. I can chose to humble myself. At this point, I may not even know how to accomplish this, but there is something I can do today. I can choose not to exalt myself.

The best way to begin is to determine how I have exalted myself in the past. This is important because my tendency is to repeat these practices again and again.

Please list seven ways you exalted yourself in the past.

DAY FIVE

I put aside my wants and desires.

5 Often my attempts to exalt myself rise from my wants and desires. Something must be mine, so I assert myself and my will in order to acquire this thing.

What have been some of your recent acquisitions?

....
....
....
....

What are some of your current wants and desires?

....
....
....
....

This is a crucial day because this is the day the path becomes steep and challenging. Can you feel the path rise when I ask you, are you willing to put aside your wants and desires? Many wants and desires are part of the problem because they easily engage the self that wants to be exalted and held high.

Today I simplify my desires.
Join me in declaring once in the morning,
once in the afternoon, and once in the evening,
I desire the humble life.

Day Six

I acknowledge my powerlessness.

6 It is not enough to declare that I want the humble life. Admittedly, this is an important step, but so is releasing my many desires and wants. This steepens the path, but it is the path I am to walk. See how quickly the promise of effortlessness calls for effort?

Now the path steepens again. Ahead there are times of rest, times when the yoke will be easy, but not today. Today, I acknowledge my powerlessness. I believe that every spiritual discipline that truly leads to oneness with God is founded on powerlessness.

For instance, powerlessness is integral to the program of Alcoholics Anonymous. These seekers are often asked to name the many things in their lives over which they have no power. Alcohol is obviously one of the first things they list, but there are many others.

I spent years helping alcoholics in their quest for spiritual understanding and breakthrough. Many of these men and women shared their deepest and darkest secrets with me. They also told me of the spiritual practices and disciplines they were putting to work in their lives. One of these practices helped me, and I am sure it will help you as well. It is your activity for today or as long as it takes you to complete it.

List one hundred things over which you have no power.

....
....
....
....

A Forty Day Guide

....
....
....
....
....
....
....
....
....
....
....
....
....
....
....
....
....
....
....
....
....
....
....
....
....
....
....
....
....
....

Please review the list of things
over which you are powerless.
As you look at each item remember:
Powerlessness often reveals the power God is.

DAY SEVEN

Through humility, I am sensitive to spiritual forces.

In the past, a feeling or acknowledgment of powerlessness frightened me. I felt out of control and at the mercy of conditions and people. Now I am beginning to see that there is another possibility. When I feel powerless, it is possible that I may experience a power greater than myself.

It is strange, but powerlessness and humility are akin to one another. Humility and a feeling of powerlessness allow me to be sensitive to spiritual forces. In the past, powerlessness caused me to center upon myself and my fear. Now I know I have the opportunity to be sensitive to spiritual forces. They are nearer than hands and feet because they are a part of me.

I may not feel powerless today, but I can pause and be sensitive to my surroundings, seen and unseen.

Let this be your work today.
I suspect divine power will be more real before you sleep tonight.

DAY EIGHT

I willingly form a partnership with God

8 I am powerless, and God is the only power in the universe. The wonder is that the Presence desires to form a partnership with me. In a way that I do not understand I must be part of the divine plan. Could it be that Spirit needs me? One thing is certain, I need Spirit.

I joyously enter into partnership with my Creator. I will do my part while knowing there is little I can do. And yet, I sense I am vital to the alliance.

Please consider that you are being offered a partnership with God. Why would a powerless being be offered this alliance? At the end of the day, please indicate what you have discovered about powerlessness and your role in the divine plan.

DAY NINE

I give the gift of my attention to another person.

Today the path of humility is less steep. In fact, there is a beauty to this day I will not forget. It begins because I forget myself. I do this by giving the gift of my attention to another person. This will help build a consciousness of humility in my soul.

For too long, I have been the center of my universe. Now someone else will take center stage. This is a two-day project. Today's work is to determine who I will give attention to and how I will give this attention.

Please indicate the person's name and what you are going to do. Tomorrow, Day Ten, you will give the gift of your attention and record not what happened, for that is not important. Instead, record what you felt.

DAY TEN

By giving the gift of attention to another person, I am humbling myself.

10 By giving the gift of attention to another person, you humble yourself. In fact, focusing upon anyone other than yourself is helpful. Remember as you complete the final day of this two day project that you are moving farther along the path of humility. With each step, your soul is more open to the touch of the Divine.

Please record your feelings and experiences below.

....
....
....
....
....
....
....
....
....
....
....
....
....
....
....
....
....
....
....
....

DAY ELEVEN

Wisdom is evidence of the touch of the Divine.

11 The touch of the Divine blesses me in many ways. One possibility is wisdom. This was Jesus' experience when he knelt and wrote in the sand as the religious leaders asked him what should be done with the woman caught in adultery. From Jesus' humility came the words, *"Let him who is without sin among you be the first to cast a stone at her."*

Today, I open myself to divine wisdom and guidance. As I do so, I realize that I cannot make an insight rise up from within me. Such an effort would be exaltation. Instead, my primary work is to remain sensitive to the thoughts moving within my mind. The touch of the Divine is often gentle and subtle, and I do not want to miss the blessing that could help another person or transform my life.

It is a good practice to be aware of the thoughts and feelings that move within me. Some, of course, originate in my human consciousness and are of little value, but others are a divine blessing.

Today is a day to watch and observe your inner world of thought and feeling. Too often the outer world is all we know. This is not enough for a spiritual being, nor is it wise because there is a vast kingdom within us. Please write of your experience. If insights come, write them in a simple, clear manner. Years from now, you may return to this page and find that what you have written helps you with a situation you are facing at that time.

....

....

....

D A Y   T W E L V E

I cease trying to gain God's love.

12 Sometimes I am so busy trying to gain God's love that I am unable to feel the love that is perpetually showered upon me. The danger is that I will falsely believe that I am not loved.

What are some of the ways you have "tried to be good," so God would love and bless you? Please list three.

....

....

....

The truth is I am loved. Love is my nature because I am made in Love's image. Therefore I cease trying to gain what I already have. Instead, I devote time to being still and experiencing the everlasting love of God.

Today's activity is a joy. Simply ask in prayer this question, God, do You love me? Become like a child, ask the question, and then listen with your whole being. Please record any insights that come to you.

....

....

....

....

....

....

....

....

DAY THIRTEEN

There is no such thing as personal power.

13 In the past, I believed strongly in personal power. Now, I am entertaining the idea that personal power does not exist. However, I cannot say conclusively that I believe the affirmation for today—there is no such thing as personal power.

I have passed through several stages of understanding regarding power. The stages reflected the circumstances of my life. First, I felt powerless, and therefore it became important to have power and dominion over my experiences. Power meant security, control, and peace. Later, I encountered circumstances over which I had no control. I was back to powerlessness again. There was nothing that I could do. From this hapless state came a deeper understanding of power. God is the only power in my life and in the universe.

Do you recognize the stages of understanding regarding power? Have you come to believe there is no such thing as personal power? If you have, please write to me and tell me about your discovery. (I can be reached at the address for Inner Journey found at the end of the book.) If you do not yet comprehend the nature of personal power, complete the forty day guide, and then write to me about your emerging humble life.

DAY FOURTEEN

Humility's foundation is one Presence and one Power.

14 Humility's foundation is that there is only one Presence and one Power in the universe and in my life—God. Many people would argue against this statement. There appear to be many powers active in the universe and in their lives. Perhaps the key word is appear. There *appear* to be many powers. . . .

I have never read about or witnessed a humble person arguing with someone about this idea, but I have seen and read about people who live as if God is the only power and presence. Their lives become expressions of Spirit. Power, creativity, and compassion flow from within them. They treat others as if they are divine beings. All life is sacred to them.

Rather than try to intellectually understand today's affirmation, I am going to put it to the test. I am going to treat the first person I meet today as if he or she is a spiritual being. Also, I am going to treat the person I spend most of my time with today as if this one is also God's creation, an expression of the Presence.

Why don't you do the same?
Perhaps together we will discover that humility's foundation
is one Presence and one Power.

DAY FIFTEEN

I am a servant of divine power.

15 I will not investigate the kingdom of God with my intellect. Thinking is a wonderful gift of Spirit, but it cannot take me where I want to go today. I must live as though there is only one power in the universe—God.

I do this by no longer trying to wield power or be powerful. Instead, I am willing to feel the touch of the Divine and to become a servant of Spirit.

This will be a day filled with many pauses. All my actions will have a prelude in which I silently declare my willingness to be a servant of Spirit. This I do not for my glory, but so Spirit will have an avenue through which to express itself.

In the space below write how many times you were able to comply with today's request. Did you have an awareness of a power greater than yourself at work? If you did, what was it like? Was there strain or did you work effortlessly?

....
....
....
....
....
....
....
....
....
....

DAY SIXTEEN

When I am powerless, God can be the power in my life.

16 Being powerless used to be the last thing I wanted. I had enough of that feeling and experience years ago. Being powerful was a logical way to put that way of life permanently behind me. The difficulty is that when I believe myself to be powerful, I do not allow God to work in and through and as my life.

Can you remember a time in your life when you felt powerful as a human being, yet out of touch with Spirit? What were the signs of this experience?

....

....

....

....

....

Now consider a time in your life when you felt powerless. You did not know what to do, so you ceased your efforts and turned to God. This moment was God's opportunity. What happened?

....

....

....

....

....

DAY SEVENTEEN

My purpose in prayer is not to gain God's favor.

17 Today begins a new journey in prayer. No longer do I view prayer as a way to gain God's favor. This favor has taken many forms in the past. I have wanted a healing, a job, peace of mind, a relationship. On and on the list goes.

I now realize that there is no humility in this kind of prayer. There was a continuous mantra—me and mine, me and mine.

Is this the prayer you have prayed? Has the object of your prayer life been your life? If this is the case, you have prayed without humility. In the days to come, we will put a new kind of prayer to the test. In less than 25 words express your willingness to pray with humility.

....

....

....

....

....

....

....

....

DAY EIGHTEEN

I admit my prayers have lacked humility.

18 I admit my prayers have lacked humility. I have been willful and hoped to express personal power and gain personal possessions. Through the years, I have prayed for hundreds of things for me.

What have you prayed for and not received?

....

....

....

....

....

....

The day will come when your prayer will have only one answer—an awareness of the One. You will ask for God, and Spirit will answer your prayer by revealing to you that It lives in you. Please consider that the humble life grows in the stillness of silent reflection. Before you retire this evening, ponder the truth that the Presence lives in you. You may already believe this truth, but now is the time to consider how this understanding can change your prayer life. How can it prepare you for the touch of the Divine?

D AY N I N E T E E N

Today I change my intent in prayer.

19 If I were solely a human being, it would be understandable that my prayers be about the human world in which I live. Satisfaction and fulfillment would require that my outer world be harmonized. However, I am a spiritual being, and because of this, I find no true solace or fulfillment in that which lies outside of me. Only a full awareness of what I am and of the One who created me can satisfy my soul.

It is for this reason that today I change my intent in prayer. I no longer bring my outer world into my prayer life. Instead I hope to come to know the kingdom that rests within me. I long to see that God dwells in my inner world.

Scripture encourages me to ask, and so I ask for the one thing that has been offered to me which I have failed to ask for: God. My prayer is simple. God, dear friend, I ask for You, to know You, to experience Your Presence. This is enough for me.

Let this be your prayer this evening. Speak or think these words, and then be still. Listen, reflect, and be sensitive to the touch of the Divine. This is a prayer of humility because it puts aside the human experience and opens the soul to a divine experience.

DAY TWENTY

I pray in humility today.

20 I pray in humility today knowing that there is nothing I can do to bring about an experience of the Presence. Prayer teaches me the nature of powerlessness, and therefore it opens me to the power that God is.

Today there is no asking for anything for me, not even an awareness of the Presence. I am simply present, turned Godward without expectation. It is enough that I give myself to Spirit. Finally, there is no desire for me or mine. There is no aspiration that something happen to me or even within me. I pray in humility knowing there is only God.

Please read today's lesson four times: in the morning, at mid-day, in the evening, and just before your time of prayer and meditation regardless of the time of the day or night.

DAY TWENTY-ONE

Humbly I wait.

21 The heart of prayer and meditation is waiting, not words or thoughts. How can a transformation of my consciousness occur if I am so busy speaking and thinking that I do not allow Spirit to have Its way with me.

The challenge is that waiting is not easy. When I am still and cease my active role in prayer, my mind wanders. This humbles me. My only recourse is to accept my meandering mind and its journey from one thought place to another.

When my mind meanders, I watch where it goes and what it values and considers to be more important than a relationship with God. I return to the pure intent to know God, and I wait again. In the course of prayer and meditation, this process is repeated over and over. I give attention to Spirit. I wait. My mind wanders, and I watch its meandering without judgment. I come home again to the Presence.

Put this prayer method to the test. Wait and be humbled, for from this humble place will come the only true form of exaltation—an awareness of God.

DAY TWENTY-TWO

I listen for the prayer that God is praying.

22 For years I have assumed that God was listening to my prayers. Now I know that I should have been listening to the prayer that God was praying. For most of my life, prayer has been what I do. Now I am considering that there is more to prayer and meditation than the words I speak, the truth I affirm, or the spiritual practices I utilize.

Prayer is an awareness of the Presence. I have tried, but I can do nothing to awaken myself to my Creator. This humbles me, and this humility teaches me that knowing God is an act of grace. Awakening is God's work, and God work is prayer. So today I will wait and listen to hear the prayer that God is praying.

As you continue to give yourself to the forty day guide to the transcendent life, record any "prayers" that you have "heard" God praying. They may be simply statements like I love you; fear not, I am with you, or this too shall pass. Please realize that often God's prayers are sensed as feelings such as joy or peace. Even an image can be the prayer that Spirit paints in your soul.

DAY TWENTY-THREE

I am willing to embrace the unknown.

23 Humility is being willing to embrace the unknown. It is also an act of maturity, for who truly knows what even the next moment will bring? The unknown and mystery are always before me, but I have tried to avoid them by taking the known path.

Today, do a new thing even if it is something as simple as driving a different route to work or reading a book on a subject with which you are unfamiliar. The point is step into the unknown. This is a humble act because there is no security in it. What did you do?

DAY TWENTY-FOUR

I see through the eyes of a child.

24 When I was a child, there was a freshness to life. I was awestruck by the stars at night, but now I seldom even lift my head to see the sky at night. Today, I will look at life and my environment through the eyes of a child. The first thing I will do is observe my surroundings and describe some part of it from the viewpoint of a child. I will use words that are important to a child and a part of a little one's vocabulary. For instance, a child might describe cumulus clouds as marshmallows or say that trees are shaped like lollipops. The difficulty will be to truly focus on something that a child would value rather than something I find interesting.

This is your work today, to allow yourself to be awestruck. What did you decide to view from the vantage point of the child? Were you awestruck? If you were not, why not? Has your intellect or supposed understanding stripped away the mystery of life?

D AY T WENTY-F IVE

Mystery walks the path of life with me.

25 I may think I know the direction of my life, but I do not. In an instant, my life can change. A telephone call, an accident, meeting someone for the first time, or reading a book can change me forever. My problem is that I fail to acknowledge that mystery walks the path of life with me. In fact, I have tried to live without mystery.

I set goals for myself and pursued them with great vigor. The goals gave me direction, and they were a way to take control of my life. If everything I wanted to happen came into being, I would not have to face the insecurity of mystery. I now see that where there is no mystery, there is no humility. Where there is no mystery, there is no faith.

Pause several times during the day and look around you. You may be in your office or perhaps outside sitting in a park or in your backyard. Look around and silently say to yourself, mystery is here; mystery walks the path of life with me.

DAY TWENTY-SIX

When I am humbled, I humble myself.

26 I have been humbled many times. It has happened in athletic events, in relationships with people, with my children, on the job, etc. I must admit that I did not like being humbled. I did not see it as a new beginning. In fact, I resented it. Because of this I failed to humble myself. I failed to admit my mistakes and limitations. In many instances, I tried to build defenses and make excuses for my behavior. Sometimes I could not even say I was sorry.

Whenever I acted in this way, even the power of the universe could not lift me up. This has been my experience, but now I am trying to live differently. It is not always easy, but I know that if I humble myself after I have been humbled, there can be a new beginning.

Saying I am sorry and admitting my mistakes take maturity. What I once resented is now seen as a way to begin anew. To fail to humble myself is to fail to enlist the aid of a powerful friend that can illumine me and assist me in living. No longer will I push aside this powerful ally, the Spirit of the universe.

When was the last time you were humbled? Did you humble yourself? If you did, what did you do or say? If you did not humble yourself, how would you react differently today? What would you do?

....

....

....

....

....

Day Twenty-Seven

An awareness of God is exaltation.

27 Many people believe there are many forms of exaltation. In an earthly sense this is correct, but true exaltation is an awareness of God. This has been an important discovery for me. I had been so oriented toward my earthly life that I tended to think that a blessing was something that happened to me rather than in me.

Now I am beginning to see that true blessings are those that touch and enliven my interior life. This is where my relationship with Spirit grows and transforms me.

So today I do a new thing. There may be wonderful things that happen to me. I will not diminish them; I will give thanks for them, but I will also remain sensitive to the blessing that is a deepened awareness of the Presence that indwells me. This is exaltation that lasts forever because it becomes a part of me.

As this day begins, remind yourself of a great truth by writing today's affirmation in the space below.

....
....
....
....

As the day ends, once again write the same statement. In this way, a circle is drawn that declares an awareness of God is exaltation.

....
....
....
....

DAY TWENTY-EIGHT

Unforgiveness is a root of discord in the world.

28 Unforgiveness may be the root of discord in the world, but it is also the root of much pain and suffering in my life. How easy it is to justify the hurt I am experiencing by blaming the pain on another person. This is has been my human tendency for years. However, my spiritual tendency is to love.

It is true that another person may treat me with disrespect, but the pain I feel comes from more than the person's actions or words. The thoughts I think about the situation or person cause a reaction within me. This unforgiveness is the root of my pain.

This realization brings me hope. I recognize that I am not helpless and do not need to endure the discomfort forever. Because the root is within me rather than the other person, I do not need to feel helpless. I can be free.

Is there a situation in your life that is hurtful? If there is, briefly describe it.

....

....

....

....

....

Do you believe that the origin of the hurt is within you rather than the other person's actions? If you are willing to embrace this idea, write a statement that expresses your willingness. This is enough for today because tomorrow you will take a step that takes you deeper into forgiveness.

DAY TWENTY-NINE

There is no forgiveness without humility.

29 Yesterday, I took an important step toward being free of the hurt and pain of unforgiveness. I took responsibility for what I was feeling. I ceased blaming the other person for my pain. This is quite different from my previous attempts at trying to free myself from resentment and anger. The step to be taken today is just as vital as the previous step.

Today's action rises from the idea that there is no forgiveness without humility. Righteous indignation or being right may help me justify the way I am feeling, but they do not free me from my pain, so I take the difficult step of humbling myself. I assume that what the person said about me is correct. (Please note that this approach to forgiveness is not always appropriate because the action may not have been something someone said. However, continue with the exercise in order to determine its validity for yourself. The day may come when you need it.) This opens me to insights that may be helpful for my spiritual growth and allows me to look at something I may have been avoiding. It also takes me out of a defensive posture.

This is today's work. Humble yourself by assuming that the person may be correct. This approach will stir new thoughts which may promote healing. Please write any insights that come to you.

DAY THIRTY

When I forgive, I return to love.

30 The humble person works on himself, not others. I have found this to be true. My previous approach was to work or to want to work on the other person. If I could only change him or if he would only apologize, I would be free of the hurt. I discovered that this path to forgiveness was a detour that never led me to love.

Forgiveness is a return to love. It is expressing my true nature. This begins when I cease trying to change the other person. The greater challenge is whether I can release the love that is within me while the person continues his inappropriate behavior. This is the challenge of forgiveness and why it is so difficult.

This understanding stresses more and more that the healing must take place in me, not the other person. This was Jesus' point when he was asked how many times we should forgive another person. His reply was seventy times seven. When I no longer demand that a person change, I have returned to love because love never demands change. Love accepts people the way they are.

If there is a person who is challenging you now, this individual may seem to stand between you and your return to love. If this is the case, silently think the following idea whenever a thought of the person enters your mind. I no longer demand that you change. I accept you as you are.

DAY THIRTY-ONE

I am aware of the ego trap.

31 Of course I am aware of the ego trap. I have spent years in it. Whenever I seek the approval and praise of others, I am in the trap. There is a tendency to try to gain favor through service to others. This is one of the most insidious snags along the spiritual path. A person can spend a lifetime in the ego trap and not know it.

There will be signs along the way that I am in the trap, but they are often ignored because I am convinced that "greatness" and approval come from other people. This, of course, is not true. I am looking to others for something God has already given me. The challenge is that the longer I look to others for praise and approval, the longer it will be before I experience God's love. This is the trauma and pain of the ego trap. It is so insidious that some people don't even want to leave it. In fact, they may not be conscious that they are in the trap.

Today's work is simply to acknowledge that there is an ego trap and to ask yourself throughout the day if you are in it. Please write your conclusion below.

....

....

....

....

....

....

....

D AY T H I R T Y - T W O

I look at the intent behind my "good works."

32 Today I begin to develop a habit that I trust will be with me for the rest of my life. It is to ask what is the intent behind my "good works." Have I come to be served or to serve?

It is shocking to consider that my intent may be tainted, but it is paramount that I know why I do the things that I do. Intuitively, I know that Spirit cannot express Itself through me if my motivation is to serve myself.

As I move through this day, I look at the purpose of my actions. If there was ever a day that called for self-honesty, this is the day.

Please list the main activities that you were involved in today. In each instance, indicate whether your attitude was self-service or service to others.

....

....

....

....

....

....

....

....

....

....

....

....

....

....

DAY THIRTY-THREE

I long to serve with no thought of return.

33 I have discovered that my intent is not as pure as I hoped. Once more, I am humbled. Now it is imperative that I humble myself. This is a difficult step, but it must be done. The question is how will I humble myself.

I will write a letter to the person I supposedly tried to serve. In this correspondence, I will admit my error and then express my longing to serve without thought of return. This letter is NOT to be mailed to the person, but it is to be written, and then read each of the remaining days of the forty day guide. Two things will become obvious. One is that intent is a crucial part of the spiritual journey, and the second is that there is a part of me that longs to serve without thought of return.

Please write your letter in the space provided.

....

....

....

....

....

....

....

....

....

....

....

....

....

DAY THIRTY-FOUR

Today I forget myself.

34 Forgetting myself is a powerful experience because, for a time, I lose an awareness of myself. In that moment, a deeper and more profound presence is uncovered. I tap into a well-spring of peace. My awareness is expanded, and I see more clearly. This has not been the normal experience for me, but I sense it is my destiny.

Today I set out to forget myself. This requires concentration or at least a supreme interest in something or someone else. I can watch a child and his explorations of his surroundings. I can listen intently to music or to what another person is saying. I can sit and observe nature and its many moods.

The key is stepping outside of my little world and becoming intensely interested in the greater world around me. This is a wonderful state of consciousness to cultivate.

Think back on your life. Has there been a time when you forgot yourself? Please describe the situation and what you experienced as the result of your self-forgetting.

....

....

....

....

....

....

....

....

....
....
....
....
....
....
....
....
....
....

How did you try to step out of yourself? Were you successful? What was your experience?

....
....
....
....
....
....
....
....
....
....
....
....
....
....
....
....
....
....
....

Day Thirty-Five

There is strength in meekness.

35 I sense there is strength in meekness. I don't know what it is, but the strength is evident. I saw it in Jesus as he stood before Pilate. I see it when people stand up to injustice, but refuse to strike out in anger or even to strike at all.

The meek endure pain, but they live their ideals and seem to accomplish what they set out to do. Ghandi endured injustice, but eventually his meekness touched the heart of those who opposed him.

Nothing appears as weak as meekness, but it has not perished from the earth. It endures and those who live life in this way are as strong as anyone who has ever lived. Meekness is like water. It appears weak, but water erodes the mountains to the sea.

Give an example of the strength of meekness. Find two examples of meekness, one from history and one from this past year. Briefly describe each one and determine what the two examples have in common.

DAY THIRTY-SIX

The meek inherit the earth.

36 It has finally happened. Newspaper headlines around the world declare: **The Meek Inherit the Earth**. Most likely the media will never affirm Jesus' beatitude on meekness, but I trust that one day people all over the world will practice meekness. This is God's way to experience the fullness of life. Through inheritance life unfolds effortlessly from a divine center.

I recall from the chapter in the book that the meek know who they are. Their identity and consciousness of self is grounded in Spirit and their experience flows from this spiritual revelation. Therefore if I am to inherit the earth, God must reveal to me who and what I am.

Spirit is always willing, but I have not taken the time to discover my spiritual identity. Today I begin anew. I rest in prayer and meditation with a simple question: God, my dear friend, what am I?

Open yourself to this revelation by asking in prayer, What am I? Please record the insight that comes to you.

....

....

....

....

....

New life begins for anyone who knows his true nature. An individual who sees himself as a human being *labors* while one who knows himself to be a spiritual being *inherits* the earth.

DAY THIRTY-SEVEN

My life flows from what I am, not what I do.

37 For many years, I focused on what I do, and this became my identity. If for some reason I was unable to complete my work, I felt less. Intuitively I knew this was not the way to live, but it was the only way I knew. Life flowed from works, therefore I strived to be as productive as possible. Many blessings came from this approach to living, but something was missing.

The meek and humble life is quite different. Works are still accomplished, but doing is not the origin of happiness and meaning. Joy and purpose flow from what I am rather than what I do. This requires an ongoing discovery of my spiritual identity. This is a never-ending journey because I am made in God's image, and God is infinite. My nature is also boundless and endless.

What will you do to begin this way of life? What will be your first step? May I offer a suggestion? Schedule a time when you can spend several days alone in a secluded place. Establish no agenda and do as little as possible. When the doing ceases, one's beingness begins to emerge. On this retreat, you will find that your life will flow from who you are rather than what you do.

DAY THIRTY-EIGHT

I am willing to inherit my world.

38 I am willing to inherit my world rather than to scramble for what I consider to be mine. In fact, I willingly release the concept of me and mine, for I now believe that there is no such thing as personal power or personal possession. Spirit is my all and my sufficiency, and my true purpose is awakening to this Presence.

This is bold and fearless work, and it belongs to the meek and humble. They are in the world, but not of it. Their earthly needs are met, but the needs are not the focus of their lives. They give themselves to Spirit, and they inherit what most of the world struggles to acquire.

This is the life that is offered to me. I have felt it to be my destiny for many years. It is time that I discover if I can live the meek and humble life. It is time to put the idea of inheritance to the test.

DAY THIRTY-NINE

Humility is not achieved.

39 I have a better understanding of the transcendent life and the underlying principles that make this life possible. However, knowledge does not assure me of humility. Even applying the principles does not mean that the transcendent life is a reality. The reason is that humility is not achieved. I cannot make it happen. It is a gift of God.

May this simple realization humble me, and may I take the next step of humbling myself.

DAY FORTY

I am sensitive to the touch of the Divine.

40 Humility may not be achievable, but it can become my spiritual path. I simply prepare myself for this harvest in the same way that a farmer prepares his fields. He knows that he cannot make the crops grow, but he is also aware that there will be no harvest unless he prepares the fields and sows the seeds. Then he waits. He waits for the sunshine and the rain. When they come, something is released from within the seeds. This unseen potential is the key to the harvest. It was always there, but something from "above" had to touch it.

It is this way with me. I am made for humility in the same way that the seed is made to grow and be fruitful. I have within me the unseen potential. Because of this, the same discovery that came to Paul will come to me. It is no longer I who live, but the presence of God who lives as me. This is the culmination of the humble life, the transcendent life. It is unparalleled oneness with God. It is the touch of the Divine.

So, dear friend, let us prepare our souls in the same way that the farmer prepares his fields. Then he watches the weather. It is interesting that there is nothing he can do to influence the weather, but he watches. Let us do the same. Let us watch for the coming of grace. Let us be sensitive to the touch of the Divine, for when it comes upon us we know humility, and Spirit has another ally with which to work Its wonders.

Journal

AUDIO CASSETTES BY JIM ROSEMERGY

Retreat Tapes

•

Living the Mystical Life Today Meditations

•

Into the Silence Meditations

•

A Closer Walk With God

•

New Species for the 21st Century

For further information contact
Jim Rosemergy at

INNER JOURNEY
PO Box 2113
Lee's Summit, MO 64063